What Others Are Saying

"On a first quick look, your book i[s...]
 - **Graham Hancock**, best-se[ller]

"Tom's new book combines his knack of explaining complex technology with his familiarity with ancient wisdom. With his step by step comparison of DNA and computer software, Tom leads the reader right to the core of great questions."
 - **Barnet Bain**, director: *Milton's Secret*, author: *The Book of Doing and Being*

"While many will find the title of Bunzel's work provocative, we are introduced to the intriguing concept of how the very fabric of biological life shares actual (not just metaphorical) principles and processes to the structure of artificial life. This ground-breaking theory forces us to reframe long-held assumptions in theology, genetics, brain science, human cognition and computer programming. This informative and compelling work expands the potential of human consciousness by asking the profound question— do we hold the keycode to upgrade humanity's collective Operating System?"
 - **Dr. Jay Kumar**, founder: *the Applied Brain Science Research Institute*

"Tom and this book's ability to bring such seemingly complex information into easily digestible material makes it a powerful tool for all readers. Whether you are turning to it for scientific or conscious understanding, it's a must read that will enhance you in both realms."
 - **Mark DeNicola**, writer & director: *Collective Evolution*

"In a provocative expression of how ontogeny recapitulates phylogeny, Tom Bunzel does something marvelous about connecting the creation of software language and the mystery of DNA. While doing this, he inadvertently gets us one step closer to appreciating the mystery of the divine in practical terms. If you've ever used the computer as a metaphor, this book is for you!"
 - **Rev. Dr. Michael Lennox**, author: *Dream Sight: A Dictionary and Guide for Interpreting Any Dream*

"In *If DNA is Software, Who Wrote the Code?* Tom Bunzel's latest book comes at a time where technology is at the forefront of the minds of the western majority. Through this literature, Tom provides us with extensive knowledge that allows us to look within our own internal programming. Not only does this groundbreaking book allows us to see that we are made up of actual software, but through his courage in sharing his own challenges, gives us permission to observe our own internal conflicts without personal judgment. I am more than proud to say that authenticity is definitely a part of Tom's programming."

- **Morgan O. Smith**, co-author: *The God Behind the God*

"There were so many parts of this book that were not only informative, but inspiring, and relatable to the point where it would be easy to see many people taking a look at their own stories and programs a lot more deeply as a result. Books like these are beautiful because it provides an outlet for those whose days are consumed by fear based thinking and mental chatter. Thank you for putting your energy and focus into something that can contribute to a global shift in a positive way. I am inspired by this information as it pertains to the future and even more inspired by the openness in which you shared your past thus leaving me in a state of awe in the present moment."

- **Christian Miehls**, director: The Vortex Dome/Meeting of the Minds Events

"Tom Bunzel has an uncanny ability to expose mind blowing ideas sitting right in front of us. By drawing connections between the known with the unknown Tom builds a complex case for imagining some of the mysterious forces animating life in simple, clear and accessible language. His writing goes down easy as he masterfully weaves a tapestry of stories and personal reflections while challenging the assumptions of our thinking without every preaching, philosophizing or imposing his point of view. Tom leads us on a tour of extraordinary ideas that will delight as it also pushes us to go deeper than we ever thought possible."

- **Terrence Gargiulo**, author: *Once Upon a Time* & *Building Business Acumen for Trainers*.

If DNA is Software, Who Wrote the Code?

The Profound Significance of Life's Programming Language

By

Tom Bunzel

Published by

Azure Reading Books

Las Vegas, Nevada

Copyright Notice

ISBN 978-0-9966240-1-5
LCCN 2015916038

Copyright© 2016, Azure Reading Books LLC
1st edition, November 2016
V1.1

848 North Rainbow Bl., Suite A111
Las Vegas, Nevada, USA 89107

www.azurereadingbooks.com

Disclaimer

It is an absolute condition of sale that you accept the following terms and conditions:

This book is legally copyrighted and protected according to the laws of the United States. All rights reserved. No part of this book may be reproduced or transmitted in any manner by any means, either mechanical, electronic, including photocopying, recording, scanning, or by any informational recording and retrieval system without express written consent from the author – except by a reviewer who may quote brief passages in a review to be printed in a newspaper, magazine or online.

Although the author and publisher have made every effort to ensure the accuracy and completeness of information contained in this book, they assume no responsibility for errors, omissions or any inconsistency herein. Any slights of people, animals, places or organizations are unintentional.

The content of the book is the sole expression and opinion of its author. This book is sold with the understanding that neither the publisher nor the author are engaged to render any type of psychological, legal, medical or professional advice.

References are provided for informational purposes only and do not constitute endorsement of any sources. Our views and rights are the same: the reader is responsible for their own choices, actions, and results.

Table of Contents

Part 1: Intelligent Life 1
    1.1 Much More Than a Metaphor 6
    1.2 What is Software? 10
    1.3 Software as Mind in Action 14
    1.4 DNA is Software 21
    1.5 HTML and Ebola – Side-by-Side 20
    1.6 Editing DNA is Now a Reality 22
    1.7 What is a Programming Language? 24
    1.8 Under the Hood of Computer Code 26
    1.9 Macros 27
    1.10 Decoding a Web Page 30
    1.11 And Now We Can Copy & Paste Life 34
    1.12 A Program is a Verb 37
    1.13 How Are We Software? 40
    1.14 Presence of Mind 43

Part 2: How Software Works 47
    2.1 Hypothetical Reality 49
    2.2 Words as Variables (God) 52
    2.3 Mystical Judaism 55
    2.4 Templates 60
    2.5 Brain Science 62
    2.6 Configuring Your Inner Startup Utility 65
    2.7 Self as Software 67
    2.8 Nutrition as Software 70
    2.9 What About God? 77
    2.10 Must the "Programmer" be a "Who"? 80
    2.11 Nature as Geometry 86
    2.12 A Modern Approach: Science v. Nonduality 93
    2.13 Life Happened How? 98

Part 3: A Shift in My Programming 104
    3.1 Rediscovering Ancient Wisdom 108
    3.2 Journey to a New Operating System 111
    3.3 Surrender... 113
    3.4 Encountering Inner Space... 115
    3.5 The Loneliness of Separation 119
    3.6 Sex as Software 123
    3.7 The Power of Sexual Imagery... 132
    3.8 Sub Space 135
    3.9 The Solace of Solitude 141
    3.10 Gambling and Numbers... 144
    3.11 That Moment When You Know You "Won" 148
    3.12 Higher Risk.. 151
    3.13 The Year of the Cat.. 155
    3.14 Accepting Not Knowing.. 159
    3.15 The Allure of Victimhood.. 162
    3.16 Russia Doesn't Exist 167
    3.17 Meditation: A Practice of Observation and Acceptance ... 176
    3.18 Doing the Opposite – Leaving the Comfort Zone 179
    3.19 There's Someone in My Head and It's Not Me................. 185
    3.20 Being the Scientist 191
    3.21 Living the Mystery... 197

Glossary of Terms 207
Bibliography & Additional Resources 211
About the Author...213
About Azure Reading Books..214

Epigraph

An Apple is an Application (.EXE)

"Because this thing codes ones and zeros, and this thing codes A T, C, Gs, and it sits up there, absorbing energy on a tree, and one fine day it has enough energy to say, execute, and it goes thump. Right?

And when it does that, pushes a .EXE, what it does is, it executes the first line of code, which reads just like that, AATCAGGGACCC, and that means: make a root Next line of code: make a stem. Next line of code, TACGGGG: make a flower that's white, that blooms in the spring, that smells like this. In the measure that you have the code and the measure that you read it - and, by the way, the first plant was read two years ago; the first human was read two years ago; the first insect was read two years ago."

-- Juan Enriquez, comparing sequenced DNA code to software at TED (2003)

http://www.ted.com/index.php/talks/view/id/80

You can certainly have Mind without logic –
But how can there be logic without Mind? ... Tom

Ask yourself, if DNA is software, where did it come from?
And then let this question seep deeply into your awareness.

A deeper look at software and DNA provides a powerful pointer to the reality of energy and intelligence as the undeniable requisite source of any encoded meaning. We can then begin to recognize and appreciate a deep and vast impersonal intelligence within the fabric of nature.

Acknowledgments

With immense gratitude to all of my teachers; too many to name:

James Kernan, Carleton Dallery, Alan Shapero, Jacob Needleman, Freeman Michaels, Dr. Orli Peter, Michael Jeffreys, Darko Juric, Michael Lennox, Jim Dreaver, Terrence Gargiulo, Michael Miller, Alfredo Ghezzi and Debra Swihart.

I am indebted to Dana J Goulston for his enthusiastic, excellent and conscientious editing of my work and to Michele Marie Blum for her cover artistry.

AUTHOR'S NOTE

Throughout this book, the reader will encounter unfamiliar terms relating to science, religion, spirituality and philosophy. Most are defined in the Glossary at the back of the book.

You, the reader are more than encouraged to contact the author should you have further questions or comments regarding anything you find interesting or worth a conversation.

Introduction

In 2008 I had a nervous breakdown; I was crying in a fetal position on my ex-girlfriend's bed while she called a friend for support.

Looking back, what made it unusual was that the year before I had had a breakthrough; I had made a deep connection between what had been discovered about DNA and what I knew about computer programming – and this epiphany had sent me back on a search for truth that had begun in my twenties.

I had revisited some teachings from my youth, studied Eastern religions and as a result everything I thought I understood, and who I thought I was, had been shattered.

After some intense therapy, a powerful group experience and subsequent research I made it back, and now I want to share the experience of what I learned to help others who sometimes feel that "they don't know who they are".

Spoiler Alert: Eckhart Tolle says that when someone tells him they don't know who they are, he says, "Congratulations."

(There are numerous references to Eckhart Tolle's work in the following pages because I am indebted to his insights for much of my recovery.)

Getting to that point for a left-brained thought-centered individual like me was not easy, but I think I have some clear markers to point the way for others who can ride my train of thought.

Let's begin ...

Part 1.0

Intelligent Life

We believe that we may one day find life "as we know it" on another world "out there."

But now that we have sequenced DNA it becomes clear that our genes represent intentional, intelligently manifested code. This "software" has been around for billions of years and yet we take this astonishing reality for granted.

Our own personal experience with apps and software from Microsoft®, Google® and Apple® can provide an important insight as to how code comes into being – and it's **never by chance**. Humans intentionally programmed all of the software we use each day.

Software is still a relatively recent human development, but we now work with it extensively on a daily basis. We simply take for granted that an inanimate intelligence is actively performing tasks according to coded human commands.

Software is clearly one of humanity's major achievements and its potential is still being discovered, especially in genetics.

If DNA is Software, Who Wrote the Code?   By Tom Bunzel

I first experienced the magic of software when I took a night job at a law firm in 1980, and their IBM® word processing system taught me how to use it – on a series of eight large floppy disks.

At the time, I marveled at how this inanimate machine could emulate our thought processes, and anticipate and respond to human input. And after I learned to use word processing software I continued to be amazed at what I could suddenly accomplish. At the law firm I could now create documents that allowed the partners to sue hundreds of people in minutes.

I also experienced my first frustrating bug, when the program wouldn't let me proceed to the next disk, even though I knew I had done an exercise correctly. I had to wait until the next day for my supervisor to reset the system in order to move on and complete the tutorial.

Later, software training became my career and I wrote about how to use graphics and video programs, and even learned to do a bit of programming. I wrote some "macros" to automate Microsoft® Office and spent a lot of time copying and pasting code, and "debugging" errors.

At every turn I was dealing with programs that "ran code". This was simply the interpretation of a set of instructions from top to bottom, left to right, in a precise order and according to specific laws, rules and principles.

Eventually like many habits, these rules and the programming itself become second nature and we respond to our cell phones, PCs and tablets like Pavlov's dogs.

Many of us who use computers, as Douglas Rushkoff has written in *Program or be Programmed*, remain oblivious to the conditioning that technology can impose, especially when we don't really understand how it works.

But if we take a closer look at computer programs we use every day, and how they operate, we can perhaps also shift our own sense of who and what we are, and what life itself is.

Consider the **fact** that our DNA, literally, operates as computer code. We can copy and paste it to give birth to another species, as biologists are now doing – or to grow new organs.

And the parallels between the genetic instruction of our physical and mental functions to computer code are startling.

If you've ever used templates in a program like Microsoft® Word® or Microsoft® PowerPoint®, you know the powerful way applying or opening a different template – or set of coded instructions – can alter the features of a document. You can instantly change the font types, sizes, and colors, along with a myriad of other attributes of the text or overall appearance of a file with another coded object, or form.

From this perspective, and noticing the different human "types" that exist, we might begin to view race as an apparent template for humans, in terms of physical characteristics, and features. This recognition of the apparent impersonal variations can enable a shift in perspective from an identification with "my" race to recognition of the intrinsic "value" of all races as expressions of a higher order of intelligence.

Focusing on our brains and the thoughts we experience, we can apply a similar perspective to memes, which are our culturally programmed mental or intellectual belief systems. Once a meme or belief is widely adopted, it is transmitted from one generation to the next through socialization and even genetics.

Using our understanding of software, we can see how our memes and widespread cultural beliefs change ... leading to our adoption of a new set of conditioned programs.

In effect, culturally, a new program is loaded into the collective consciousness.

Essentially like a new template, a cultural belief is introduced by a small group of "weirdos," who are at first ridiculed and ostracized.

Unfortunately for the people who suddenly come up with an innovative new template for human beliefs, the culture has not been kind. Think of Jesus and Galileo as two prime examples of unconventional thinkers whose ideas led to their deaths along with the persecution of "early adopters".

But if the template or meme resonates and strikes some deeper level of understanding, a shift happens … first in individuals and eventually into entire cultures.

The "Gods" may become One God (monotheism) or ultimately perhaps just the "One".

The Sun eventually is recognized as the center of the solar system.

And then remarkably we determine that our planet is orbiting a minor star on the periphery of an ordinary galaxy among billions. And now we have discovered even greater galactic motions and clusters of entire galaxies moving within incalculably vast higher patterns.

But what happens when we suddenly begin to understand the very nature of our own belief systems and templates?

We may begin to realize the arbitrary nature of our beliefs. While some may seem scientifically verified empirically, many more give way to a different interpretation when viewed impartially.

Examined in depth and with intellectual honesty we can confront the actual price we pay for many of our most cherished assumptions – and the extent to which they sometimes cause us suffering.

Eckhart Tolle's *The Power of Now* and *A New Earth* opened people up to the possibility that many of the memes and beliefs they've always taken for granted are misguided – and a new "template" was suddenly applied to millions of people's inner programming when Tolle's work was promoted by Oprah Winfrey and gained acceptance.

The highly evocative first chapter of A New Earth beautifully depicts how the very first flower suddenly "awoke" or evolved biologically, signaling a new direction for all life on the planet. Then Eckhart compares our own awakening to our true nature as a similar potential step in the evolution of consciousness.

And then we might ask, what happens when we can connect the apparent perfection of life itself (DNA and Epigenetics) with the functioning of our own inner and outer worlds and belief systems?

Might the profound realization suddenly hit us that we are not separate "things" composed of protoplasm?

Could we begin to deeply sense how we are energetically connected to a Cosmos that is itself Intelligent on a level far beyond our own—that has evolved organic life according to a set of very precise laws and intentional instructions (DNA)?

Taking into account the amazing ways disciplines like biology and physics have revealed these laws, can we now begin to drop the intellectual arrogance imposed by our scientific hubris and expand our awareness to recognize the greater intelligence at the heart of nature?

Then, by looking at the stars which seem to dwarf our existence, and a newly discovered subatomic quantum world that clashes with our common sense notions of cause and effect, can we then begin to completely reconsider what is real and what is imaginary?

That is the shift that is taking place right now.

It began for me in earnest when I saw the video by geneticist Juan Enriquez that changed forever how I saw life and reality. (See Epigraph

1.1

Much More Than a Metaphor

Before the advent of software we really had no frame of reference for the thoughts in our head–the nonstop commentary of our minds felt so compelling that we took it on as our identity.

Going a bit further, when we were able to encode our ideas in images and eventually in the printed word, the identification with our thoughts grew even stronger.

This led to the crystallization of the Cartesian world view; Descartes famously said, "I think therefore I am" – elevating thought to the preeminent human activity, and humanity itself to the apex of what is considered the highest level of intelligence or knowledge.

But it is precisely our identification with "what feels like us"– and the chatter in our heads – that has separated us from a much deeper level of truth and reality.

Now that we have encoded our mental functions in silicon and decoded the DNA within our cells as a programming language, we might open to the reality that what we experience as Mind is much more significant and ubiquitous than previously thought, and that intelligence transcends human endeavors.

"In the beginning was the Word" has an entirely new meaning in the context of software.

To begin this journey we need to first compare what we know about software to our understanding of Life – since DNA is life's software.

Recently this was impressed upon me again when I was sitting outside at a table and a fly landed by my hand. As I looked at its frenetic activity – the buzzing vibration of its wings and the rubbing of its six legs, I was struck by a very deep realization …

I realized that this insect and all life around me, including the trees and birds, were ***running the same organic operating system – DNA.***

DNA As "Operating System"

- Harmoniously Integrates:
  - Digestion
  - Respiration
  - Elimination
  - Circulation
  - And More
- Eckhart Tolle: An Immense Intelligence far greater than our minds controls these functions
- Supports the Potential Evolution of Consciousness?

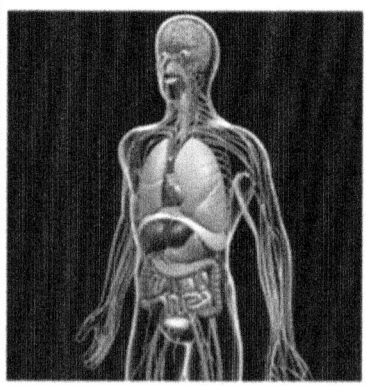

As Eckhart Tolle points out, this immense "supra-human" intelligence already exists within our bodies and brains, controlling our organic functions, without any conscious effort on "our" part.

And when one gets a deeper sense of how software actually "works" and how it is entirely based on a logical interpretation of symbols, one may begin to fathom the immense intelligence behind natural "laws".

1.2

What is Software?

At its most basic, software represents **active encoded intelligence**.

Of course humans have encoded their thoughts for thousands of years. We have the cave drawings at Lascaux, the beginnings of writing in stone tablets and even the amazing monuments at Giza (which contain no hieroglyphs) that actually memorialize encoded ancient mathematical and astronomical wisdom.

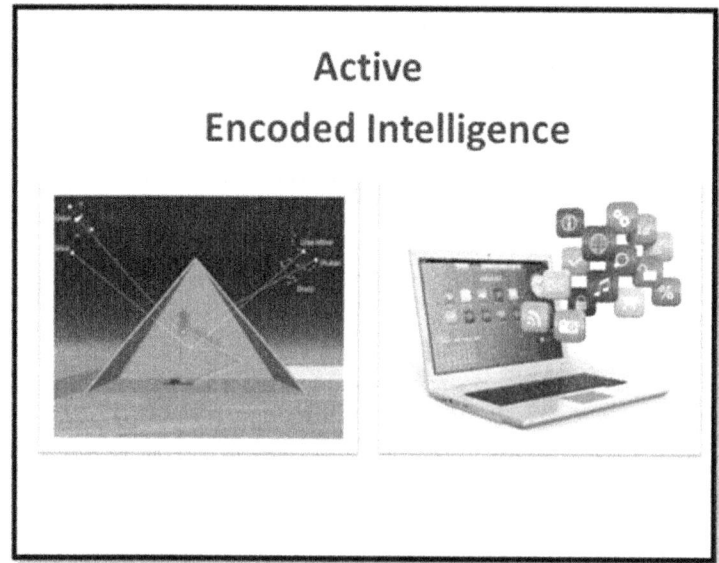

But in the 19th century modern humans took their Cartesian belief system in an entirely new and significant direction. The first calculating machines emerged and eventually there developed ways of structuring calculation to make decisions, simulations and projections.

"Charles Babbage (1791-1871), computer pioneer, designed two classes of engine, Difference Engines, and Analytical Engines. Difference engines are so called because of the mathematical principle on which they are based, namely, the method of finite differences. The beauty of the method is that it uses only arithmetical addition and removes the need for multiplication and division which are more difficult to implement mechanically."

– http://www.computerhistory.org/babbage/engines/

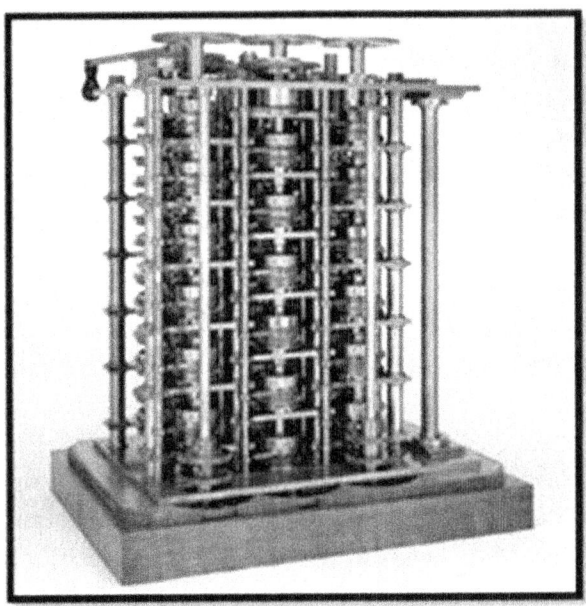

In her article in *the New Yorker* (referenced below), Betsy Moray describes how it was Ada Lovelace who first used her understanding of the potential of Babbage's machines to contemplate a new way of encoding intelligence, with symbolic logic – to create what we now call software.

She was the first computer scientist to imagine a ***programming language***.

"This science constitutes the language through which alone we can adequately express the great facts of the natural world, and those unceasing changes of mutual relationship which, visibly or invisibly, consciously or unconsciously to our immediate physical perceptions, are interminably going on in the agencies of the creation we live amidst…

A new, a vast, and a powerful language is developed for the future use of analysis, in which to wield its truths so that these may become of more speedy and accurate practical application for the purposes of mankind than the means hitherto in our possession have rendered possible. Thus not only the mental and the material, but the theoretical and the practical in the mathematical world, are brought into more intimate and effective connection with each other."

– Ada Lovelace (Betsy Moray, New Yorker, 10/15/2013)

From the same New Yorker piece: "[Charles] Babbage's system – the engine, Lovelace explained, weaved algebraic patterns. She also wrote how it might perform a particular calculation: Note G, as it is known, **set out a detailed plan for the punched cards to weave a long sequence of Bernoulli numbers, and is considered to be the first computer program**.

"'The science of operations, as derived from mathematics more especially, is a science of itself, and has its own abstract truth and value." Lovelace wrote.

Lovelace also saw the connection between the scientific language she just conceived and the quality of mind that has always seemed uniquely human: "'What is Imagination?' Two things, she thought. First, 'the combining faculty,' which 'seizes points in common, between subjects having no apparent connection,' and then, she wrote, 'Imagination is the Discovering Faculty, pre-eminently. It is that which penetrates into the unseen worlds around us, the worlds of Science.'"

The software that Lovelace imagined – which would "flower" a century later – added a new dimension to encoded intelligence. It was now potentially **active. *It performed tasks.***

(It is also possible and quite likely the megalithic structures of antiquity were "hardware" in the modern sense, because their design encoded knowledge that energetically provided power or other benefits for their populace. The pyramids might have actually also been "running software". We get into this more deeply later and there are references in the Bibliography).

1.3

Software as Mind in Action

During the 20th century, when the Nazis used the IBM Hollerith machines to tabulate and sort the Jews and dissidents for transport, the notion that Lovelace suggested – that such a programming language can "*adequately express the great facts of the natural world*" were not yet contemplated. Holleriths were the offspring of Babbage machines and were basically calculators; the Nazis licensed IBM software to make them work and awarded Thomas Watson, IBM CEO, their highest honors.

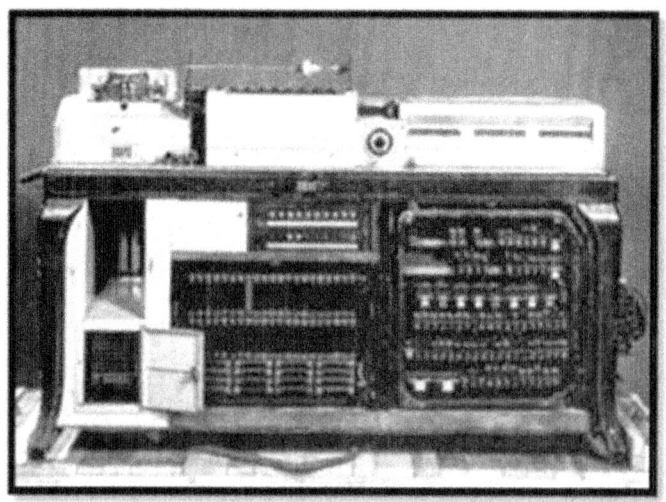

If DNA is Software, Who Wrote the Code?   By Tom Bunzel

The first theory about software as potentially intelligent – prior to the creation of personal computers as we know them today – was proposed by Alan Turing in his 1935 essay *"Computable numbers with an application to the Entscheidungsproblem"* (the problem of decision-making).

Notice how this already contemplated actual artificial intelligence; the ability of a machine not only to calculate, but to actually make decisions and with stored memory, learn from its "experiences".

This can be simplified, for now, as the If-Then syntax of programming. Based on the evaluation of a set of known parameters ($A=X$) one of two (or more) outcomes can become "programmed" or determined.

Of course Turing is known for his famous "test" for artificial intelligence in which a subject is given the chance to try to discern whether his interaction is with a human or a machine. If the subject cannot tell the difference, then the machine is deemed "intelligent".

But all of these early efforts were based on the assumption that the logic of the computer is purely human and that our propensity to think in such linear ways is what separates us from other beings. What we may discover is that intelligence is not a uniquely "human" property – and that purely linear thought is a relatively low level of intelligence.

Even when the computer became "personal" and individual users could customize their own programs, its connection with our intimate biological functions remained unknown.

Not until DNA was sequenced by supercomputers and its logic "exposed" as simply a much more complex set of instructions to be carried out – not by electronic circuits in silicon – but in our tissue, cells and blood with proteins, hormones and other chemicals, was there the chance to begin to make a deeper connection.

But bear in mind, no programming language from the time of Lovelace until the present ever "evolved" spontaneously from inanimate objects; instead it was ALWAYS the mental product of an intentional intelligence (humans).

Lovelace even imagined the future of graphics; the nascent conceptual beginnings of what we now call virtual reality are actually based on her suggestions for a weaving loom (that followed her program) to create geometric designs and color patterns in fabric or carpet.

So it is really only in the last 200 years or less that modern human ingenuity could faithfully replicate nature, so as to begin to emulate the workings of our own Mind or Consciousness.

The first computers as you may recall used punch (or punched) cards:

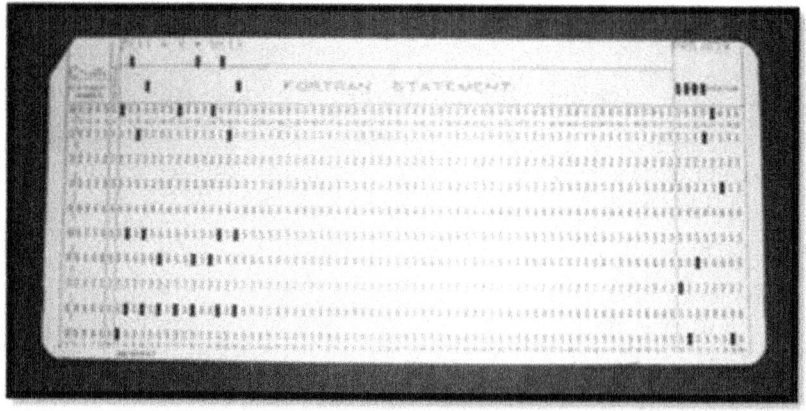

– https://en.wikipedia.org/wiki/Punched_card

And even then it is uncanny how similar this looks to this image of our chromosomes from the Human Genome Project:

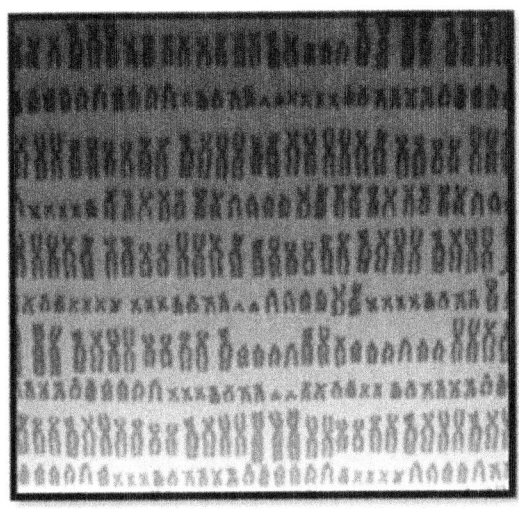

– Popular Science 2010: http://www.popsci.com/science/article/2010-03/future-genetics-computing)

In this article in Popular Science in 2010: *According To Genomic Pioneers, The Future of Genetics Is The Future Of Computing*, it was contemplated by the Human Genome Project's creator, Craig Venter, that "Without a means to process, analyze and cross-reference all that information, we would simply be floating on a sea of base pairs and phenotype data with no practical means of navigation. The need for such an analysis could be the best justification for building a proposed 'exascale' supercomputer, which would run 1,000 times faster than today's fastest computers."

So even our most powerful supercomputers were incapable of navigating through the complex maze of data of a single Genome in sufficient time for geneticists; and the future of computing and the future of genetics are inextricably intertwined.

We can now contemplate quantum computers (based on the "intelligence" in subatomic particles) and the possibility of using the technology of DNA for storage. Nanocomputers based on Quantum Physics and at miniature scales that defy comprehension are also in the works.

And this also brings up the fact that science has discovered that the "hardware" of DNA can actually be used to store massive amounts of human-created information more efficiently than our own "artificial" memory devices.

Might this begin to suggest that perhaps computers were created "in our image" – either consciously or unconsciously – and essentially "evolved" based on our mimicry of our own intrinsic nature?

When we begin to recognize the parallel between the encoded intelligence we create as software, and its timeless presence in our own being, we can begin to fathom the reality that … DNA **IS** Software …

1.4

DNA is Software

Now we can look more directly at what geneticist Juan Enriquez says about DNA in the TED (Technology, Entertainment, Design) video referenced in this book's Epigraph.

He draws a direct connection between the code in our cells and a floppy disk.

Holding up a floppy disk and an apple, Enriquez says: "Because this thing codes ones and zeros, and this thing codes A T, C, G's, and it sits up there, absorbing energy on a tree, and one fine day it has enough energy to say, execute, and it goes thump. Right?

And when it does that, it pushes an .EXE [Executable], what it does, is it executes the first line of code, which reads just like that, AATCAGGGACCC, and that means: make a root Next line of code: make a stem. Next line of code, TACGGGG: make a flower that's white, that blooms in the spring that smells like this. In the measure that you have the code and the measure that you read it – and, by the way, the first plant was read two years ago; the first human was read two years ago; the first insect was read two years ago."

– Juan Enriquez: *comparing sequenced DNA code to software at TED (2003)*

1.5

HTML and Ebola – Side-by-Side

Enriquez also shows a slide with the source code for the Ebola virus.

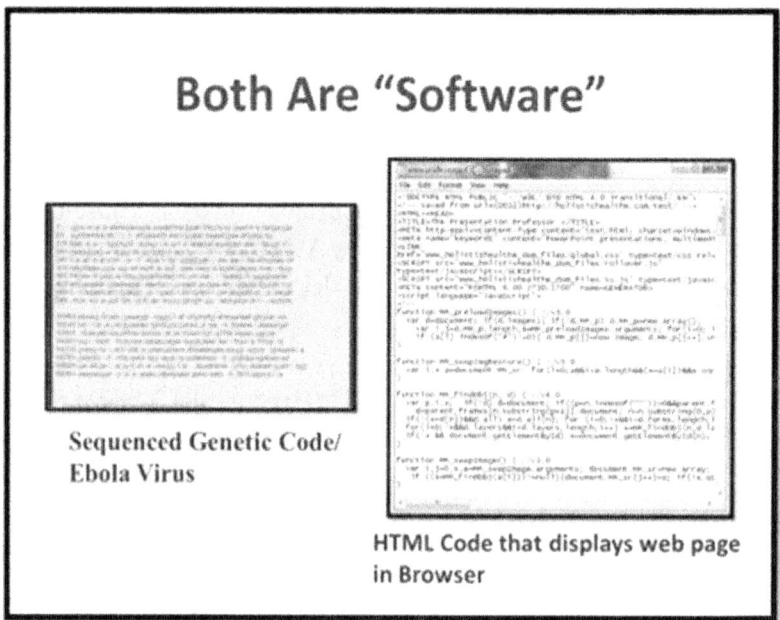

If you look closely at the Ebola sequenced DNA code, it appears as a series of four English letters – *AATCAGGGACCC* – referencing proteins that will act biochemically according to the coded instructions.

Perhaps most significantly, Enriquez never says that DNA code is "like" computer code. For him there is no distinction; operationally; they are identical, functioning on pure logical statements that are read top to bottom – left to right.

His parallel is precise. It is "the same as this floppy disk": a storage device for the immensely complex coded instructions that manage our biological processes.

1.6

Editing DNA is NOW a Reality

As I write this news has emerged of the newly developed CRISPR-Cas9* method for Genome editing in living organisms – a powerful new technology with many applications in biomedical research, including the potential to treat human genetic disease.

Paul Knoepfler, a stem cell researcher at UC Davis (University of California), describes CRISPR as a molecular Swiss army knife: "It's part Genome scanner (like a magnifying glass tool on the knife), part scissors to cut the DNA, and part pencil to re-write the genetic code."

– LA Times

This is yet another indication that "DNA is software" – not metaphorically behaving "like" software but literally and objectively another form of encoded intelligence.

As I write this "MIT biological engineers have created a programming language that allows them to rapidly design complex, DNA-encoded circuits that give new functions to living cells.

"Using this language, anyone can write a program for the function they want, such as detecting and responding to certain environmental conditions. They can then generate a DNA sequence that will achieve it.

"'It is literally a programming language for bacteria,' says Christopher Voigt, an MIT professor of biological engineering. 'You use a text-based language, just like you're programming a computer. Then you take that text and you compile it and it turns it into a DNA sequence that you put into the cell, and the circuit runs inside the cell.'"

– phys.org

What does this mean?

Well, for anything **to be edited it must convey meaning**; the concept of editing is simply revising its essence or meaning.

And this can only be accomplished within a consistently intelligently behaving system with predictable patterns.

You cannot "edit" randomness or chaos. By definition chaotic changes occur randomly and not predictably.

There is no "order" without Mind.

*Clustered Regularly Interspaced Short Palindromic Repeats, and CRISPR associated (Cas).

1.7

What is a Programming Language?

It is probably more accurate to refer to DNA as an "**organic programming language**".

When one views HTML – the programming language of the Internet – the code is in English.

The instructions written in the HTML programming language simply tell a web browser how to display text and graphics.

HTML's instructions are comprehensible commands in a language we understand. On the electro-chemical level they are then "translated" into the machine code that lets the silicon chip perform the magical calculations that make the web page appear in another software program (the web browser) and finally on our screen via colored and organized pixels.

The color displayed by each pixel is the result of more code; as we will see there is an RGB (Red Green Blue) numerical value for each color that is read by the web browser.

Does it really matter whether the symbolic language is in English or in protein?

Remember that in decoding DNA we (arbitrarily) assign the letters A, C, T and G to represent the protein building blocks (called bases) that perform the biochemical tasks instructed by the code – again these are the organic functions that regulate all of our bodily (and also our mental) functions.

What might this begin to suggest?

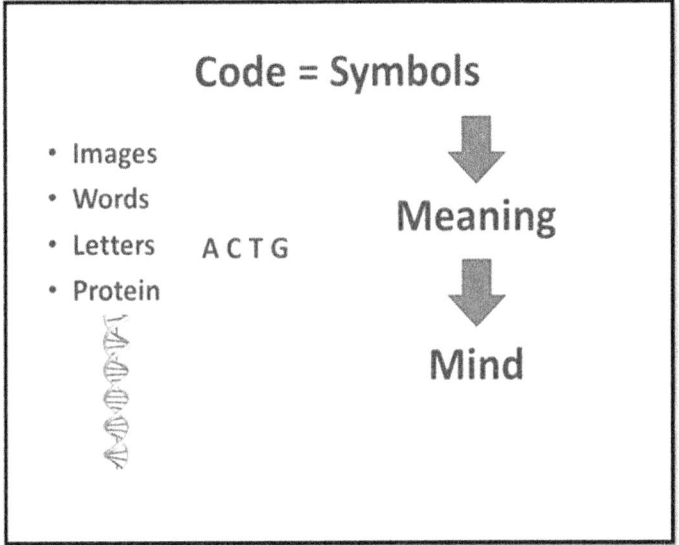

A=Adenine
C=Cytosine
T=Thymine
G=Guanine

1.8

Under the Hood of Computer Code

At this point let us look more closely at the code that performs the tasks that we know so well – the actual software that works in our cell phones and PCs.

Perhaps by more closely examining the code we use every day, in surfing the Internet or creating documents and presentation, we can gain a more profound understanding of what it means that there is code running in our own bodies.

1.9

Macros

A Macro is a "subroutine" or snippet of code in a program like Word® that does something when it receives input – a keystroke or mouse click.

A macro is a very simple but powerful coded "object" that performs a task, emulating precisely the techniques and logic at work in much more powerful programs – like Word® itself (which is "creating" this document") or an actual operating system that creates an entire working environment in a computer that runs Windows® or software from Apple® or Google®.

Remember again Enriquez's description of the apple – its code is activated by energy from the sun. The end user's movement of a finger activates a macro. Both actions represent a simple input command or mouse click. As you read through the following simple snippet of code you can now get a sense of how Word® creates a Red Rectangle.

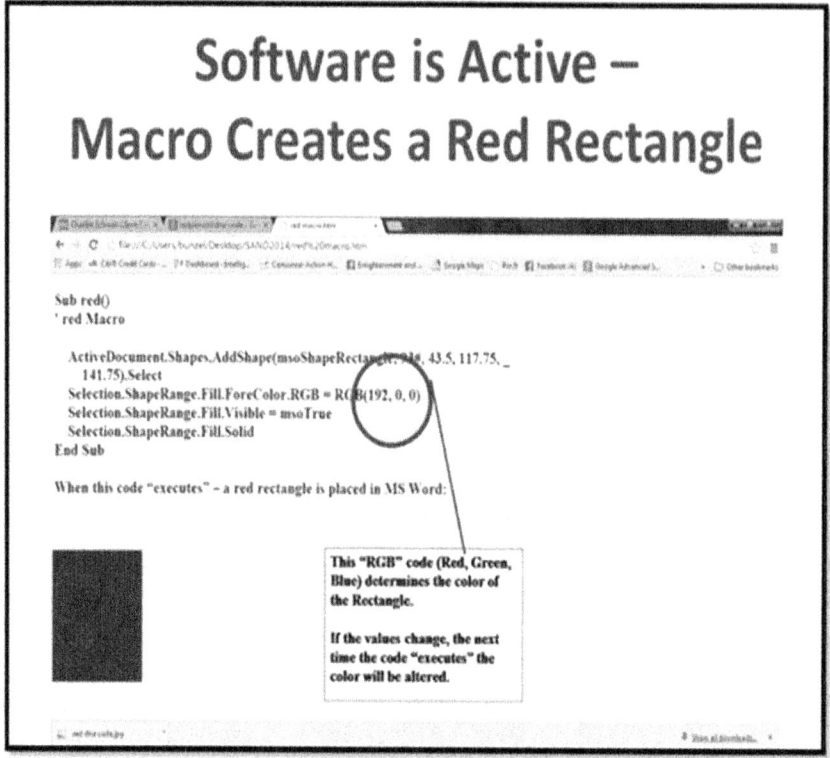

Notice that within the "**Active-Document**," the mouse input generates a series of subsequent commands:

First is the process of "selection" and then the addition of attributes or properties:
        1. Make a rectangle;
        2. Make it red.

Enriquez: "… pushes an .EXE, what it does is, it executes the first line of code, which reads just like that, AATCAGGGACCC, and that means:
1. Make a root;
2. Next line of code;
3. Make a stem;
4. Next line of code;
5. TACGGGG;
6. Make a flower that's white;
7. That blooms in the spring;
8. That smells like this."

In the previous greyscale figure, the color Red is represented by an RGB (Red-Green-Blue) series of numbers or values. By changing the numbers to represent blue, the next rectangle created by a mouse click would be that precise shade of blue. (RGB values range between 0 and 255 – black is no value – white is all values.)

1.10

Decoding a Web Page

In the HTML code (Hypertext Markup Language) that "expresses" as a web page, the programming language is just a bit more complex, but with a bit of "decoding," it can also be easily understood:

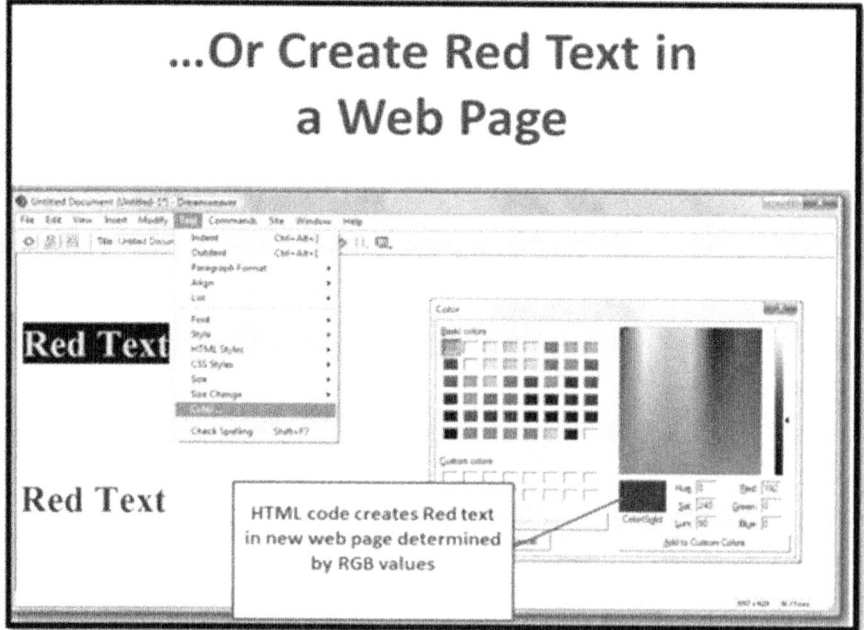

HTML code creates Red text in new web page determined by RGB values

You can see this for yourself by right-clicking "View > Source", or "View page source" in most web browsers:

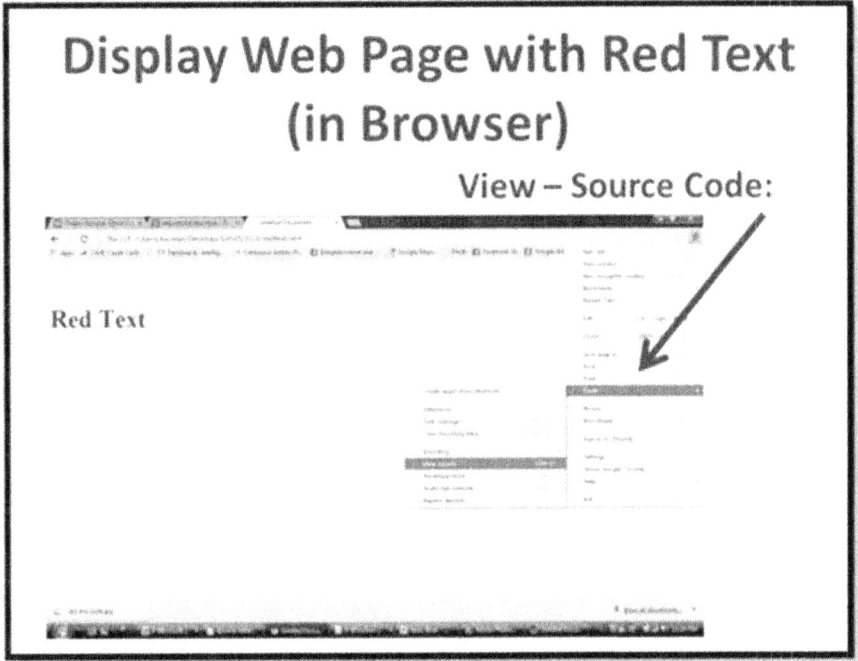

In each case the expression of Red can also be "decoded" to a numeric value. Remember that the Red Rectangle in the Word® macro expresses according to a very specific RGB value.

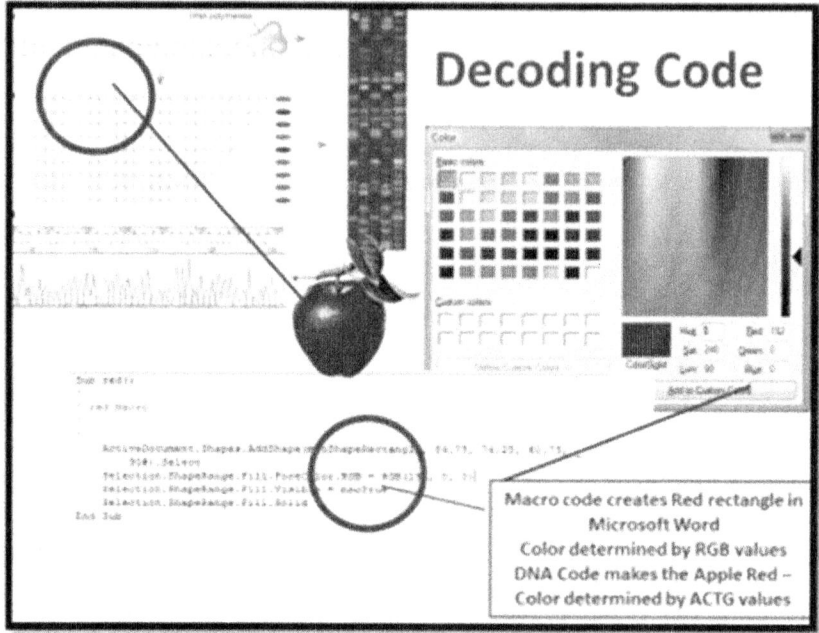

In a web page's HTML the coded value is simply part of a different system (set of laws) known as a "Hexadecimal":

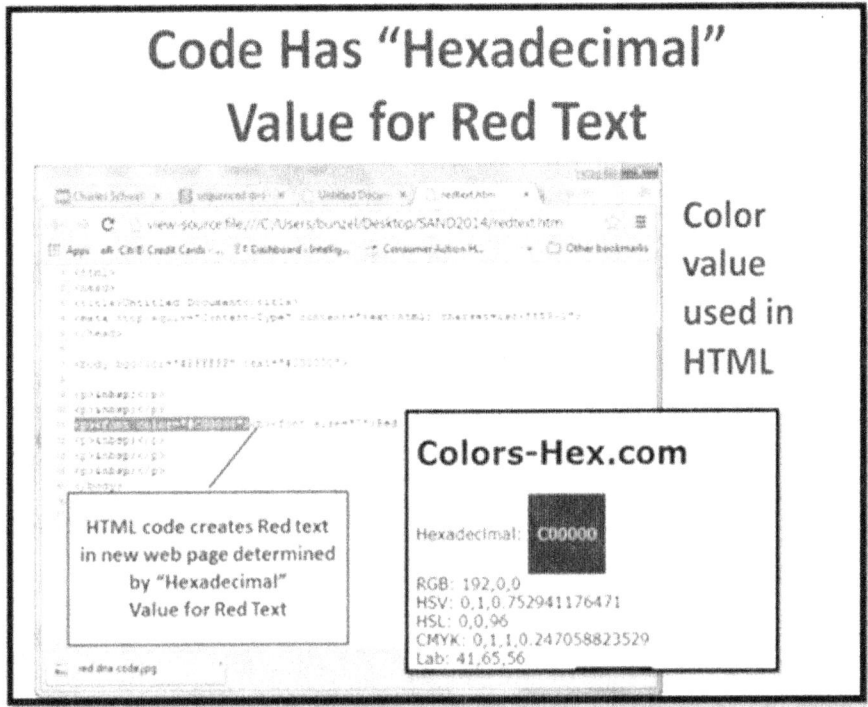

The system for encoded intelligence is basically irrelevant – all systems (to be successful) must merely operate with complete logic and consistency (something akin to "intelligence").

With DNA the code executes as chemicals and we simply reference their activities in the sequenced code with the letters A. C. T and G – as shortcuts to the specific proteins that do the "work" – or actively express the code's intent.

We now are also beginning to understand that these operations are not wholly determinative or "set in stone" – genes express in harmony with the environment (the emerging science of Epigenetics).
But let's continue our inquiry …

1.11

And Now We Can Copy & Paste Life

Just as Juan Enriquez describes the birth of a baby gar, an animal that was almost extinct, by putting its DNA into the egg of an animal that is still living, we've done the same thing in Word®.

If you've copied and pasted text in a word processor, or copied a picture to put into another document, you have performed the same function yourself, twice – once by selecting the coded object that was to be moved or copied, and once by "pasting" (or simply repeating) the underlying code as you performed the operation.

In both cases you were just manipulating a group of symbols.

Because DNA is Software...

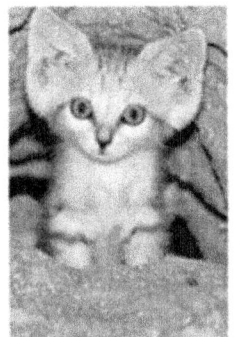

Copy DNA an endangered Arabian sandcat into the egg of an ordinary house cat and just as the code in the web page shows the video in the blog, the egg now produces a sandcat instead of a housecat.

-- Sixty Minutes with Leslie Stahl

http://www.cbsnews.com/videos/resurrecting-the-extinct/

We can "Copy and Paste" Life

Here is the relevant portion of the article about the Sixty Minutes piece: On the day we visited, they were laparoscopically removing eggs from an ordinary housecat, and then sending the eggs down the hall to have the housecat DNA sucked out of them.

"What she's doing is she's removing the DNA from this domestic cat egg. And she can see it by what we call fluorescing it," Dresser explained, while observing the procedure with Stahl. "It becomes just very blue, and so now she knows where it is. And now you'll see her go in there and be able to remove it."

Once the housecat DNA is deposited outside of the egg, they will replace it with the DNA of an endangered Arabian sandcat, a completely different species, gathered from a tiny piece of skin.

"And there you see it being inserted into the domestic cat egg," Dresser explained.

"And you made that from just skin?" Stahl asked.

"Just from skin cells, right," Dresser said.

An electrical impulse starts the egg dividing, and if all goes as planned, the now sandcat embryo will be put back into the domestic cat to grow to term.

Of course that is how some scientists believe "life began" – **but where did the source code come from?**

This is particularly mysterious when you realize the true nature of a program.

> *Points to consider: If wireless networks communicate invisibly and powerfully then why should Mind be any different? We now know it's just "information" – zeros and ones in the wireless network.*

When Eckhart Tolle is asked what we actually are, he says "no thing." What better description of wireless technology and Mind can there be?

1.12

A Program is a Verb

When I taught software skills one thing I tried to explain was the difference between a program and a file. A file, like a Word® document or web page, is a thing or a noun.

A program (or application) on the other hand has the amazing capability of changing the environment or more simply put creating or "editing" a file.

(In terms of personal experience this may resonate if you consider the need to safeguard or "back up your work." Backing up files (or things) is very easy – you just copy or move them to another storage device.)

Originally the simpler versions of programs like Word® or Excel® could be moved the same way – you could just move the "executables" (word.exe) files.

But as the programs grew more powerful and complex, particularly with respect to graphics and video, they needed to "reinstall"; that is coordinated more deeply with an equally complex operating system that "understood" personal identity, preferences and other parameters.

Word® creates, edits and prints "things" – files and documents (or uses macro code for other functions, as we just saw). Google® Chrome® or Microsoft Internet Explorer® take HTML code and display a web page according to the rules of their systems, or "programming language".

This places a program in a unique position in the field of encoded intelligence; almost like a musical composition in the hands of a conductor, an application works in concert with an end user and peripherals to achieve a goal.

And without the intelligent guidance of a programmer (or conductor) our software would not function. And without the (intelligent?) input of the sun (DNA) or an end user (computer software) nothing "happens."

(Later we will also consider how Epigenetics has now expanded the seemingly deterministic view of DNA to include its interaction with the infinitely vast other energies in our environment).

And remember a program (or application) is not an object. It is a subjectivity – always doing and changing.

Another important aspect of understanding software emerges when a program does not "work correctly" and we call tech support.

Think about the "aha" moment that comes so often after a frustrating experience where we anticipated a program performing a certain way, and then get an alternative explanation that suddenly "makes sense" from the perspective of the programmer.

A "setting" that we had neglected to pay attention to suddenly "solves" the issue.

The system as designed was perfect. It was our understanding of its functioning that was flawed.

What this always indicated to me (after I calmed down) was that another (person's) mind (in contrast or different from my own) had used a thought process or progression to create or code the program that was beyond my comprehension. After this was clarified, suddenly the entire process "made sense" but it required a shift in perspective.

This might become very relevant to modern sciences like physics and biology, which seem to be dealing exclusively with nouns and oblivious to verbs.

1.13

How Are We Software?

When it is cryptically suggested that we are software it may seem as though the reference is simply to the stream of seemingly intelligent (random or intentional) thoughts in our head.

> *Don't our thoughts, as Descartes suggested, serve in some instances as our inner operating instructions?*

In some ways these conceptual, symbolic representations of reality or life may be the "work product" of software in our own brains, in the same way that a Word® document is the result of the word processing program that creates it.

But Word® the Software is not a thing – but rather a subjectivity – moving and active creation tool that can perform intentionally devised tasks.

And remember that by far the majority of functions taking place in our bodies are not "conscious" – if we had to remember to breathe or circulate our own blood (pump our heart) we would not be alive. They are regulated by the code running in the nucleus of our cells.

But Word® (or web browsers that display HTML like Internet Explorer® or Google Chrome®) or **all of the other software** with which we're familiar was "designed," written or programmed by a huge team of specialists.

Many programmers were writing the code and others strategizing and testing it, and of course distributing and marketing the program. But again, the program is not a noun but a verb – it does things on a screen or on paper based on an intelligent and consistently devised system.

If we now recall what Buckminster Fuller said, "I seem to be a verb" we might begin look into our own biology and with discernment and depth start to see something more than a collection of "things" or organs.

And bear in "mind", (pun intended), one of these organs, the brain, which seems to be the thinker and the little man inside my head generating thoughts is actually a hub of chemical activity that represents the "hardware" of consciousness. But what makes us "tick" and what (or perhaps "who") we are is the software.

And in terms of constant change or energetic activity, consider that no cell in your body at this moment was there when you were born, and that by the time you finish this sentence, your body will have changed significantly biochemically even from when you began reading.

There is also absolutely no evidence where or how the brain initiates and creates the energy we experience as thought, or any other sensation or *experience*. Rather the brain is the switchboard for the immense network of intelligent energy that permeates our bodies, and those of all living things.

You are no more your brain than a quarterback or a point guard is the team. Even if with the analogy of an individual sport like boxing, thinkers like Dr. Ravi Shankar have pointed out the impossibility of isolating and identifying, for example, exactly "when" and "by whom" a punch is thrown. Did the shoulder launch the punch, or the brain, or an instinctive circuit trained during previous weeks in the gym, or the "input" of the opponent?

And remember too that you are not consciously either choosing your thoughts or running your biology. How often, if ever, do you (or can you) choose your next thought?

And again all of your most critical bodily functions are being harmoniously controlled by a greater system that makes sure you breathe, excrete, ingest, circulate your blood and, yes, even think. Who exactly, then, is "in charge"?

And if it's still 'you' is it the "you" reading right now, the "you" going to work tomorrow, or sleeping with a loved one? In each case the you that manifests is clearly influenced and evoked by those you are with, the food you ate, and the entire ecosystem and environment where the experience takes place.

This is the essence of the new science of "Epigenetics" being furthered by thinkers like Bruce Lipton, Deepak Chopra and Dr. Rudy Tanzi. Your genes are no longer seen as "determining" your activity or nature; rather they switch on or off (express) based upon a much wider field of intelligence that we refer to as the "environment".

And where is that? Simply here. Sure you are on earth, but where exactly is that? Think about it.

The earth seems solid and stationary; but we know that it is moving rapidly around a rather ordinary star, which is itself encircling a vast galaxy in a scale of time that we can barely comprehend.

And then perhaps we might look a bit deeper and begin to question who, exactly, is it that is thinking?

1.14

Presence of Mind

Software is logic instructing silicon – DNA is logic instructing proteins, neurons and Life – **both require the pre-existence of Mind.**

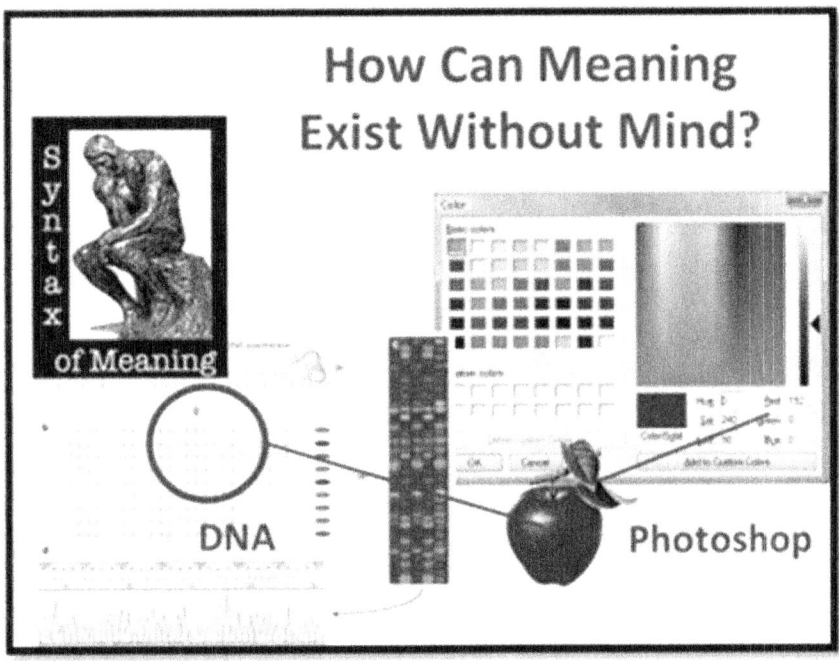

Just as Microsoft®, Google® or Apple® software would not exist without a monumental mental effort, it is illogical to suppose that the obvious intentional intelligence behind DNA could have "evolved" from inanimate matter.

Software is Encoded Intelligence

No computer program has ever appeared by accident; Google, Apple and Microsoft use teams of programmers to produce lines of code

Going back to the very beginnings of software, whether it was Ada Lovelace, Charles Babbage or the designers of the pyramids, their intentional machines running software were always created and operated by sentient beings.

There are current movements like *panpsychism* that suggest that all matter is alive and potentially sentient depending upon the vibration of its subatomic particles. But even in this case, the active nonmaterial component – the energy or perhaps the space between material components – would need to be software – or the mental aspect of its existence and functions.

And also remember that our own software is deemed to be "intellectual property." By this we clearly don't mean the paper or screen on which the information is stored but rather the intrinsic value and potential use of the "information" itself. It's "think stuff" not "thing stuff".

And the very notion of "information" suggests or even posits a Mind. For anything to have meaning or order there must be Mind as an organizing principle, or by definition, it is chaos.

And let's remember that for the information to have "value" there must be an entity – an intelligence – that comprehends and interprets it. Who might that be for DNA?

For now the interpreters are geneticists but they have merely decoded (and sometimes revised) an **organic programming language** that has existed for at least four billion years.

And the letters A, C, T and G which we have arbitrarily assigned to represent the proteins that actively carry out the instructions of DNA are not the software but rather simply represent, or act as "placeholders" for an as yet unknown, but obviously immense intelligence behind it.

Clearly we have no claim on this immense intelligence. It certainly preceded us, it may have created us, and it is certainly far more intelligent and complex than our own mental capacity has thus far discerned; remember that it takes a supercomputer to decode.

So what is operational within our own cells, and represents our own living instructions, is a set of encoded intelligent conceptual imperatives that got there before we arrived and are operating right now inside you, without your conscious knowledge, even as you read this.

There can be no "information" without Mind.

Information is an overlay of order onto chaos by the mind. To the extent that information can be discerned actually existing in nature, nature must be intelligent.

This is the profound significance of DNA being decoded as software – and all other scientific discovery.

Then also consider the many pieces of "information" that must remain forever hidden to us if we not create the instruments (or have the biological capability) to discern them.

"No things" like Wi-Fi and all other radiation – immense swatches of the electromagnetic spectrum – may still be beyond our comprehension.

Therefore Mind or Consciousness must of necessity be the next domain of valid scientific inquiry – if possible.

Part 2.0

How Software Works

If/Then – Causal or Psychological?

Having established that DNA is a program based on encoded instructions, let's continue to examine how that works in computers.

In this way we can model or gain a different perspective on what may be going on with "us".

One of the most powerful and common "statements" in computer programming is If/Then.

"If Income > $50K (greater than $50,000) approve the applicant's credit card."

But having discovered logical programming syntax in our DNA, which controls our bodily functions, can we also infer that we have the capability to make decisions using our brain – which presumably processes the information made available to us by the environment?

From a purely logical perspective this would seem to imply that we may have "free will." If I can see a condition and act accordingly then I would seem to be "free" to make the choice.

We have to examine this question more deeply.

Just as we have seen genetics (originally a deterministic model) give way to Epigenetics (a much more complex model of interactive energetic reality of which we are a tiny part), so too is neuroscience currently unable to locate a single "self" as a controlling agent behind the eyes.

Nondual teacher Wayne Liquorman has a wonderful quote: "If you think you have free will, use it".

To me the entire notion of free will/determinism is broadly conceptual – neuroscience and philosophy have never been able to identify a single root "cause" that inevitably leads to an effect – the presumed cause can always be shown to be part of a much larger set of influences that trace back to – the Big Bang (yet another concept).

I prefer to consider that perhaps there is an infinite reservoir of "will" (intelligent energy) by which to choose but none of that is "yours" – but paradoxically all of it is You.

(For more on the neuroscience note the references to the work of neuroscientists Douglas Hofstadter and David Eagleman, and later on).

And yet the inexorable logic of the organic programming language of DNA is at work, as we have seen in nature, in the Enriquez video – (if conditions permit) "make a root, make a flower, etc."

And similarly, in the web form for applying for credit – if conditions permit (appropriate income greater than $50K) – issue a credit card.

So the question becomes, who exactly would be the one "acting" in accordance with the program?

And perhaps further, where exactly (and when) does the intelligence required to make a "choice" reside?

Hint: Before simply responding, "in the brain, duh," let's probe a bit deeper.

2.1

Hypothetical Reality

The If/Then sequence is clearly a big part of our survival programming: (If I walk into the jungle will I get eaten?) but there is one problem: it can lead our body to respond whether the event has taken place or not.

Neuroscience has discovered that the body stores stressful memories and it doesn't really discriminate whether those memories or thoughts are the result of stories or actual events occurring in the present moment.

I remember beginning to work with my teacher Michael Jeffreys and noticing how I was starting to fret over a dentist appointment weeks in advance. I was already anticipating the discomfort and loss of control and yet nothing had actually occurred.

It wasn't until I began to practice not believing my thoughts, talking back to them, and just allowing them to float by, that I was able to wait until I was actually in the dentist chair to react naturally. And by that time my stress level had subsided dramatically and I could accept the actual discomfort (as compared to the incremental accumulated discomfort hypothetically presented to "me" by my thoughts).

If/Then is great in a web form or a Word® document ... "If I select this text and click BOLD, I will change the formatting."

But it can have absurdly powerful consequences if not understood as *a hypothetical reality.*

In one of our group meetings someone challenged some of the ideas by asking, "What if an earthquake hit right at this moment and a giant crack opened in the floor? How would all of this acceptance stuff work then?"

Some of us chuckled nervously but the point was made even before the response came from the front of the room: our mind loves to create situations that give it attention. But since no earthquake was **actually happening** the purely hypothetical nature of the question was exposed.

But what if you live in fear of losing your savings? "If the market crashes, I will be left homeless." This is a profound example used by Eckhart Tolle who describes the moment the phone rings, the broker tells you the value of your portfolio, and you proclaim, "I'm ruined."

Eckhart uses this example to show the power of the hypothetical mind to project outcomes that, left unexamined, can lead to horrible misery.

There was a story of a billionaire who lost much of his fortune and was left with "just" $100 million and committed suicide. Our assumption that our thoughts are what is "real" can lead to dire consequences.

Very helpful in this context is the "Work" of Byron Katie, which has a four step process for analyzing such hypothetical or even actual situations, but ultimately it comes down to two issues:

Is the issue really true? Is the market crashing? Is there an earthquake?
And in interpersonal situations she will ask, "Is it true?" and then do a "turnaround" which reframes the issue from the other person's perspective.

Seen "impersonally" the issue is often transmuted with the recognition that truth is relative. A person may begin to see that what they experienced as betrayal, for example, was another person just being who they were – the result of their own patterns and conditioning.

Suddenly something that was hurtful and "personal" is seen impartially as making sense – it's another form of "tech support." Seen from an equally understandable but "other" perspective, the hurt can subside as truth enters into our being.

And most important is this question that Byron Katie asks: "Who would you be without that thought?"

Taken in deeply, beyond the mind and into the body, this powerful query will strip almost any thought of its power.

Once it has been identified as a hypothetical fantasy that may or not be valid, the energy behind the thought will dissipate and a sense of spaciousness can allow for other possibilities to unfold.

At bottom is the recognition that the "one" we take ourselves to be is not a fixed, static thing, but rather an energetic presence that is constantly changing and adapting – a variable of sorts.

It is immeasurably helpful when we apply this same line of inquiry to questions about religion or God.

2.2

Words as Variables (God)

But what if we begin to think in programming terms of God as a "variable" – essentially a placeholder for the concept of "I Don't Know."

Ironically, or perhaps coincidentally, the name for God in Hebrew is "Adonai" – it almost sounds like "I don't know."

So how does a variable work in software? The programmer can "declare" a word as a variable – for example – *First_Name* might be declared as a "string" variable (holding text) so that when a visitor to a web site fills out a form, the word "First_Name" holds the value he or she types in, so that First_Name = John or Mary.

Another type of value that can be declared as a variable is a number. So then when the user fills in his or her age or date of birth, the number is "contained" in the variable ("Age"=X) and entered into the program as it "runs" (lives energetically as a manifestation of programming intention).

Now Age may equal 44, or 32, or 90. It is a matter of its interaction with the end user, or in the case of DNA, with the "world".

In a web form, for example, if Age is less than 18, hopefully the user will be denied access to a page of pornography.

This is the same principle which applied logically above – if X (the variable holding the value for income) was greater than $50K, the applicant receives a credit card.

Incredibly we now know that DNA operates just like computer software, conveying meaning through a set of symbols that work in organic molecules instead of silicon chips.

But to me, this process of manifesting an idea energetically through an intelligent set of instructions suggests that something profoundly significant is happening in all organic life – something blatantly obvious but which we have overlooked and taken for granted.

We are quite literally the manifestation of an idea or very complex set of concepts; or to put it in terms that are eminently understandable only today – "software."

Epigenetics has expanded our understanding of DNA so that we now know that if we replace the genetic code within a cell – the energy that expresses itself through those instructions continues to operate and now expresses as a new species with different properties.

Perhaps an entirely new template has been applied – a new set of features and properties are now expressed biologically but underneath – the intelligence that is being expressed is the same. This provides a startling insight into the equality of races.

We saw that with the baby Gar in the Enriquez video, and the Arabian sandcat in the 60 Minutes piece the genetic code was changed. The energy expressing through the code (irrelevant to most biologists except someone like Dr. Robert Lanza who coined the term "Biocentrism") is presumably the same.

This has made it apparent that our DNA does not determine us, but rather the ways in which our genes "express" is a function of their interaction with the environment according to energies we are only now beginning to acknowledge and comprehend.

Therefore, what happens to "us" is the result of forces or energies flowing through us – including our thoughts and patterns of conditioning, which create "inputs" that switch certain genes on and others off.

So that what is in effect "natural" becomes not just the result of materialistic determinism, but rather part of a much more complex and in fact "intelligent" or "intentional" set of processes which we still barely understand – and which of course modern science ignores.

The instruction set (DNA), in its very manifestation of meaning, points to a higher level of intelligence – not just more complexity.

This reality – call it Mind, Consciousness or God, has proven very inconvenient for conventional science.

What are we to make of the undeniable FACT that programming, similar to what we have created in "its image," is at work within our very cells?

Where and what is the energy behind such a process? Is an understanding even possible solely (or "soul-ly") through the intellect? Or does it require a measure of contemplation, reverence and awe for something Higher?

Religion has been the means by which these "transcendent" realities have been addressed in human history – until the advent of science – which is merely another current meme, or religion.

While many may follow ancient religious rituals by rote, others may be moved to a sense of something deeper and far more profound – which is currently only on the periphery of scientific inquiry.

But there have always been clues.

2.3

Mystical Judaism

During my sophomore year of college, I decided to attend Yom Kippur services to please my father, and we were denied entry because we had not ordered tickets. We were banished to a basement as "second class Jews." My father was incensed, and when he later retired in La Jolla he told me that his synagogue became the beach, the ocean, and the sun.

He had a very difficult life, and he attributed his survival to a faith in something higher. I have spent a great deal of my life seeking the same level of peace by searching for meaning – or something Higher – intellectually.

I investigated the mystical aspects of Judaism by attending some lectures on Kabbalah, and noticed a tremendous resonance between its teachings and the concepts of eastern religions that talk about a conscious awareness at the root of life.

This is said to lead to knowledge that is beyond the intellect; that needs to be felt with the heart.

This leads us beyond our current preoccupation with an intellect "housed in the brain" and is a common theme in ancient cultures. (The image below is the Kabbalah "Tree of Life" symbol.)

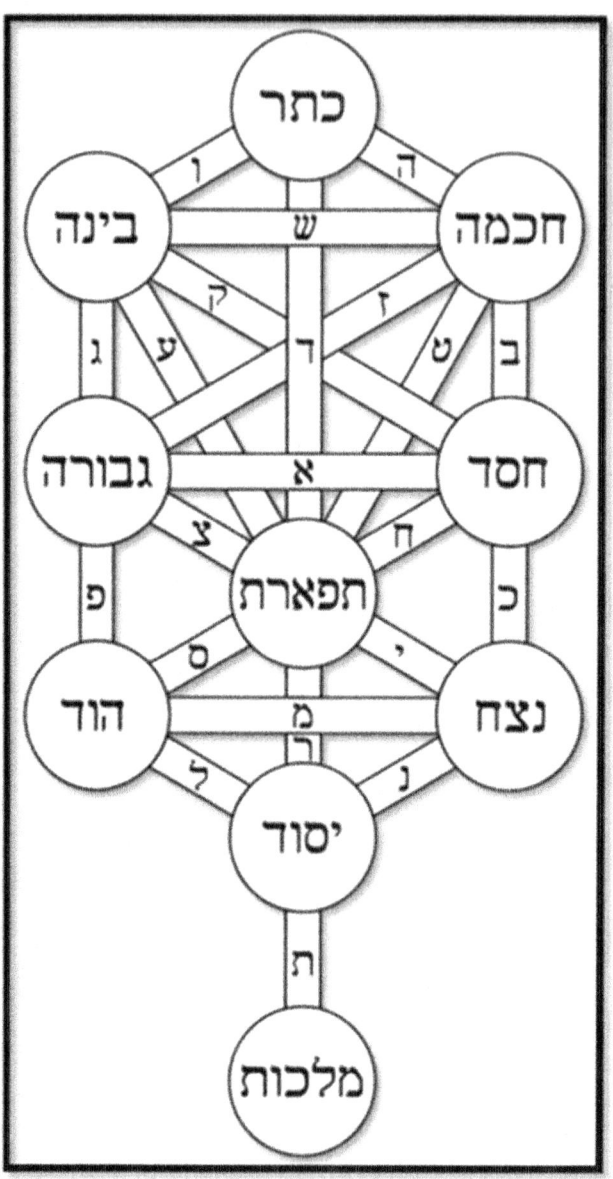

Here is Wikipedia's description of the three levels of the human soul according to Jewish mysticism:

"The Kabbalah posits that the human soul has three elements, the *Nefesh*, *Ruach*, and *Neshamah*. The *Nefesh* is found in all humans, and enters the physical body at birth. It is the source of one's physical and psychological nature. The next two parts of the soul are not implanted at birth, but can be developed over time; their development depends on the actions and beliefs of the individual. They are said to only fully exist in people awakened spiritually. A common way of explaining the three parts of the soul is as follows:

- *Nefesh* (נפש): the lower part, or 'animal part', of the soul. It is linked to instincts and bodily cravings.
- *Ruach* (רוח): the middle soul, the 'spirit'. It contains the moral virtues and the ability to distinguish between good and evil.
- *Neshamah* (נשמה): the higher soul, or 'super-soul'. This separates man from all other life forms. It is related to the intellect and allows man to enjoy and benefit from the afterlife. This part of the soul is provided at birth and allows one to have some awareness of the existence and presence of God."

The question arises, how does one connect to such a higher level of soul – once one suspects or acknowledges its existence? I was intrigued that some of the methods mentioned in Kabbalah lectures were similar to meditation, which I will get to in chapter 3.17.

And this teaching is reminiscent of many ancient teachings, including Gnostic Christianity and the concepts of Gurdjieff, and even the Egyptians.

Ancient civilizations and tales of extraterrestrials and the likelihood have long fascinated me that there have been civilizations that had a deeper comprehension of the intelligence of the Cosmos.

As I have suggested, the ability to literally "copy and paste" the symbolic meaning of Life – DNA code – from one species to another and have it express the "nature" (properties) of the donor in the host organism means that something conceptual (not just material) is moving from one into the other – the Mind or Consciousness of Life is being transferred.

And I compare this to computer software, in which the conceptual intentions of thousands of programmers can actualize energetically through a set of coded instructions.

I would approach the notion of religion or God from a similar perspective. In many cultures or traditions God is a concept that fills a deep need or void; in fact some neuroscientists have speculated that there is a "God circuit" or religious area of our brain.

Since we know that a variable is essentially empty of meaning until it is filled in by the activity of Life in the form of a computer user, can we not make the same leap with respect to any conceptual representation of a divine being who remains, at least for the moment, hypothetical?

And yet – the reality of DNA as software forces us to confront Mind at least potentially as an energy existing outside just our brains or even our bodies.

And we use such intelligence or its ability for information to be transferred without "matter" every day. We used to call it radio, then television, and now Wi-Fi.

In all of these instances we are simply moving "information" (mind stuff) – which we move as zeros and ones in our computer software and presumably in some other ways within our brains and perhaps even externally.

In fact we have experience with transferring energy both physically and otherwise in our emotional lives as well. It can be as complex as our sexuality or as simple as a hug.

I remember one of my sessions in therapy where I reached out my hand to my therapist to seal our bond of trust (I describe more of these experiences later) and made a space for our connection. I found myself saying, "I believe in wireless too," and we both laughed.

The reality that we all know is that both what we deem thought or intelligence as well as what we term our emotions are different frequencies or forms of energy. We can label them differently and thereby think we understand them but in reality their origin and transmission remain a deep mystery.

2.4

Templates

So perhaps our bodies serve as just a container for these various energies – the physical form through which they interact.

In software terminology a "form" is called a "template" – a blank (empty) blueprint for different "instances" (manifestations of coded instructions).

(Interestingly this is like a more complex "form" of variable, see above.)

A great example is in Word® where you generally use the default "Normal" template but you can create your own combination of formatting, fonts, design and so on.

Then, by "applying" or opening a different template you instantly change an "instance" – a version of the template – to reflect the programming changes.

It is interesting to contemplate how similar this is to the language of a famous philosopher who presumably knew nothing of software – Plato.

Plato, in his allegory of the Cave, suggests that our view of reality is a shadow of what is true; a mere reflection based on our sensory input that barely mirrors reality.

This myopic view of reality has been confirmed by modern science, which has expanded our sensory capacity by finding many other forms of energy beyond the spectrum of visible light.

For Plato then, the "real" Truth is manifest in what he referred to as Forms; the nonmaterial (*mental*) "abstract universals" on which he all believed physical reality is based.

I was intrigued when I heard Stuart Hameroff, renowned neuroscientist and anesthesiologist and head of the Science of Consciousness conference speak at SAND (Science and Nonduality) and suggest that it was indeed "Platonic constants" that form the basis for the seemingly intelligent programs of microtubules in organic chemistry to begin to organize themselves as living organisms.

Plato's Forms = Templates

| "Plato suggests that concrete beings acquire their essence through their relations to "Forms"—abstract universals logically or ontologically separate from the objects of sense perception. These Forms are often put forth as the models or paradigms of which sensible things are "copies". When used in this sense, the word form is often capitalized. | = | In software terms this is precisely what is known as a Template corresponding exactly to Plato's notion of nonmaterial "Forms." A concrete example of how all of organic life is programmed in our DNA (as software)? |

...so that clearly the very "instructions" for life are literally software?

Plato did not know what software was – he just understood the concept and used a different vocabulary. (Doesn't it make sense that he was describing the very true nature of DNA?)

Plato suggested that physical beings acquire their essence through their relations to such "Forms" – abstract universals logically or ontologically separate from the objects of ordinary sense perception.

("Mind Stuff")

These Forms are often put forth as the perfect models or paradigms of which sensible things are merely "instances" or "copies". When used in this sense, the word Form is often capitalized.

In Platonism, "sensible" bodies are in constant flux and imperfect and hence, by Plato's reckoning, less real than the Forms which are eternal, unchanging and complete. Typical examples of Forms given by Plato are largeness, smallness, equality, unity, goodness, beauty and justice.
– https://en.wikipedia.org/wiki/Platonism

Plato, remember, was also the harbinger of the legend of Atlantis, from which presumably his philosophical ideas may have come. Atlantis was described as a lost civilization of superior beings in the realm of science; but their science may not have been purely "objective" in the modern sense.

Rather it was said to have originally been tied to a sense of the Sacred, until like our modern civilization it became the force for domination and manipulation of nature, and perished.

Interesting great unexplained megalithic structures found recently hint at the existence of just such a civilization that was destroyed by a comet about 11,800 years ago, precisely the time period recorded by Plato.

You can read more about this in the latest book by Graham Hancock, Magicians of the Gods: The Forgotten Wisdom of Earth's Lost Civilization.

At the Science and Nonduality Conference there have been presentations by modern physicists like Menas Kafatos that are attempting to create a "subjective" or observer-based science.

2.5

Brain Science

What if instead of calling our brain and spinal cord our "nervous system" we instead referred to them as an "Awareness System"? Might that not deepen the level of our inquiry? Because our brain can also seem to "malfunction, so now we can also perhaps see such experiences in computer terms as a "bug" in the program or simply disharmony between the various systems contemplated in Epigenetics – the environment, our brain, our nervous system, and our DNA programming.

And this brings us back to the notion of "Mind" – that enigmatic ephemeral "no thing" that seems to instruct our DNA as it interacts with the environment.

For many of us, Mind = Brain, but modern neuroscience is going in other directions.

For example, when I talk to my "self", which self is speaking and who exactly is listening?

In *Incognito: The Secret Lives of the Brain*, neuroscientist David Eagleman uses this very example to raise a common question: who or what exactly is the "self" that one is always referring to?

If DNA is Software, Who Wrote the Code?   By Tom Bunzel

For Eagleman, "Mind isn't what Brain is – but what Brain does." Eagleman's recent PBS (Public Broadcasting Service) series on the brain delved deeply into the mystery of the neural network where the Self seems to "reside" but like the enormous global network we call the Internet, it is the conduit of intelligence and not its sole repository.

No self has been located or identified in a cranial region by neuroscience.

Just as our DNA software acts electrochemically, expressing thru hormones and proteins in our blood the same functions are happening in our brains and somehow, miraculously, some of those are experienced as thought.

Through thought the brain provides clues as to "what" is expressing but all conceptual models prove flawed; if we are honest the only answer is Mind or if you prefer, consciousness.

That is why psychedelics have such power – they seem to strip our conceptual belief systems away and you actually FEEL LIFE ENERGETICALLY – chemically and not intellectually and it opens, as Aldous Huxley famously wrote, the "Doors of Perception".

So how to comprehend this paradoxical conundrum because as Eckhart Tolle frequently points out, "the mind can't know the mind".

But now we do have an experiential clue as to how it all happens – especially when computer software has begun to simulate our own mental functions via artificial intelligence and virtual reality.

What better definition for it – and us – do we have than what we now understand as "software" – *intentional encoded intelligence?*

These are the instructions that we are decoding as DNA that also apparently may reveal to us the magnitude of the intelligence behind them.

Let's continue to examine the operational capacity of software for more clues as to the immensity of Mind or Consciousness.

2.6

Configuring Your Inner Startup Utility

Sometimes I refer to taking a nap as rebooting my system. As I wake up to what seems to be "normal" consciousness, my senses seem to come "on line" and I form visual, auditory and mental conceptions of the world around me – and begin to function.

When a computer is turned on, many analogous things happen as programs come "on line".

The Startup tab of the Windows® MSCONFIG® System Configuration utility lets you control which programs Windows® loads on boot up – the fewer you allow the more efficient your system and the less potential conflict (in "system memory") with "applications" like Word® or Photoshop®.

Notice that programs like iTunes® and Google® don't need to "preload" – they can be disabled and run only when needed – but they will try to load into Startup. Notice also the many programs I have disabled (unchecked) in my System Configuration …

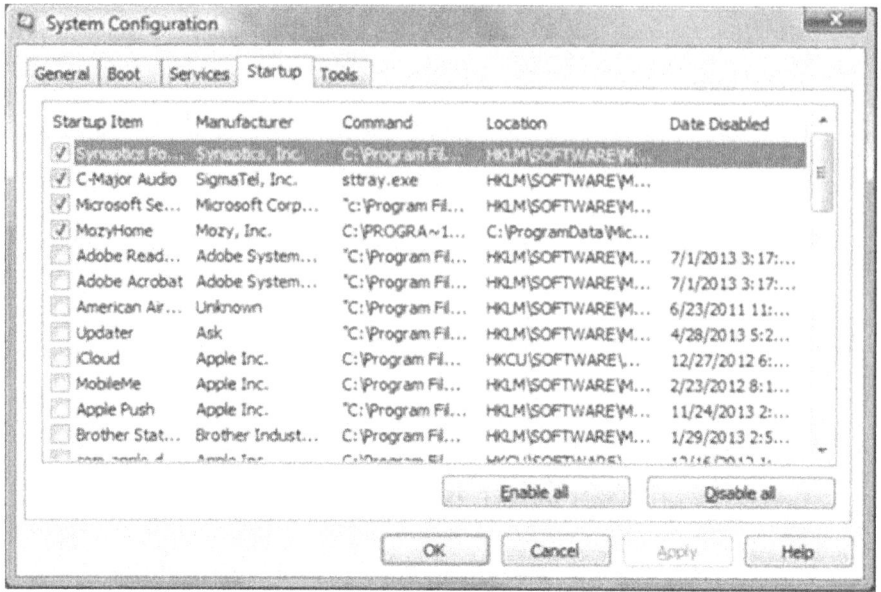

Now what about the mental processes in your brain? How many programs do you load when you wake up – assumptions, beliefs and stories that you don't need and that impede your functioning?

You can begin to notice and even disable them (in your own Startup Utility) during silence and meditation.

Meditation can help to identify unnecessary obsessive thoughts and concepts interrupting the silence.

When you just sit quietly, you can begin to notice, (but not attach to) negative sensations or feelings like boredom, impatience and frustration and then your own conscious "applications" – love, peace, harmony, family and even worldly goals can unfold more efficiently.

2.7

Self as Software

So what else do we know about software, from our own experience? Well we already know that based on written symbols (code) a different set of actions (programs) can launch and run, resulting in different sets of experiences – we see this in computer games and virtual reality – in this a way the computer simulates "human" thought.

So what about our sense of "Self"? The feeling about "us" that we take without questioning as "real"?

As noted, conventional science has long held that our "selves" are "in" the brain.

But consider this:

How could a self, soul, consciousness, "I" arise out of mere matter? Remember the words of biologist Dr. Robert Lanza – science has no explanation for how even thought or experience can emanate from inanimate matter.

In *I Am a Strange Loop,* neuroscientist Douglas Hofstadter argues that the key to understanding selves and consciousness is the "strange loop" – a special kind of abstract feedback loop inhabiting our brains. The most central and complex symbol in your brain is the one called "I". The "I" is the nexus in our brain, one of many symbols seeming to have free will and to have gained the paradoxical ability to manipulate reality, rather than the reverse.

How can [such] a mysterious abstraction be real – or is our "I" merely a convenient fiction? Does an "I" exert genuine power over the particles in our brain, or do the laws of physics helplessly push it around?

Let me digress to the teachings of a mystic and philosopher, G.I. Gurdjieff, who also suggested that we have "three brains" (intellectual, emotional and physical) and that we actually process (digest) three types of food: air (as breath), nutrition (actual "food") and impressions (thoughts/feelings).

P.D. Ouspensky, another philosopher who popularized portions of the Gurdjieff work in his seminal work, *In Search of the Miraculous*, describes the nutritional system (all three types of foods) as forming different "I's" or selves until they are integrated through intense self-observation and psychological work.

His work suggests that under proper circumstances, impressions (received through the senses) are converted into the finer energies or substances needed for Higher Intellectual or Higher Emotion centers to develop within the organism – but these conditions do not exist naturally at our current level of being.

Due to our inner fragmentation into multiple I's, or centers, the shock (insight) necessary for the proper processing of impressions is consistently thwarted by the various Ego and mental illusions that distract the organism. Our current state of being prevents and obstructs us in from summoning the consistent attention necessary for the proper processing of impressions to take place naturally.

Perhaps another way to look at this is from the standpoint of software; as a complex organism we have a main "operating system" that we consider ourselves – which "grows" as we derive our conditioned identity through our parents, peers and "education".

These belief systems form our personality, through which we are taught to evaluate and judge everything we encounter as "good" or "bad".

We develop a "personal" set of adjectives through which we function in the world and by which we continually (re)define ourselves and evaluate our apparent experience.

This conditioned personality becomes the same self about which, in his depression, Eckhart Tolle said famously said "I can't stand myself." He later used deconstruction to try to identify which self was talking and "who" was listening when he said it, and it formed the basis for both his recovery, and his famous works: *The Power of Now* and *A New Earth*.

But like modern neuroscience, and Eckhart Tolle, Gurdjieff/Ouspensky also suggest that this "normal" sense of self is illusory – comprising in actuality merely a series of Ego and mental illusions, that interfere with the alignment of our true nature – consciousness – or a proper connection to higher intellectual and emotional "centers" – and Nature or Life itself.

The various selves that we take our "selves" to be are mainly conditioned, learned patterns of thinking. Some of them load when we wake up in the morning; others are activated (switched on or loaded) when we encounter life experiences (often in the form of other people or situations) but none of them are truly "us".

We can see this very clearly in our various "roles". As we grow up we are students, then perhaps employees or employers; our professional roles give way even within minutes to our role as spouse, parent, friend, colleague or lonely bachelor.

Once again, when our selves are exposed in this way as software programs to which we give and then cede attention we are left with the question – who or what is doing (or has done) the programming?

And to what extent are "we" conscious when we go from one role to another?

2.8

Nutrition as Software

Additional evidence of the incredible complexity of who "we" are can be found by simply loading a different set of "programs" as "real food" – namely energetic input through nutrition that is "healthy".

Healthy is really just another conceptual definition for "in harmony". Ingesting the wrong food creates disharmony (or dis-ease) because biochemically our inner software program cannot process it into energy, or it actually interferes with our various programs.

I "experimented" with his recently when a friend suggested I change my diet in the morning (when I felt sluggish and negative) with a different set of chemicals listed here:

Daily breakfast shake:

- 1 banana
- 4 strawberries
- 1 spoonful blueberries
- 1 spoonful goji berries
- 1 teaspoon maca powder
- 1 teaspoon acai powder
- 1 teaspoon cacao powder
- 2 glasses of coconut water
- 1 piece of ginger
- 1 teaspoon honey
- 3 shakes of cinnamon powder.

What I believe happened as a result is that my operating system of "Self" was modified sufficiently in way where I could begin to see myself as less "separated" or differentiated from nature, and consequently more lucid and energetic.

While my DNA (software code) in the nuclei of my cells remains the same, its "activation" was altered chemically – different software is running within me.

Epigenetically I altered significant environmental inputs.

This concept of environment (Life) or energy input activating software (like a mouse click on the computer) is the new field of Epigenetics and also, as Hofstadter and Eagleman's work suggests, the current trend in neuroscience.

The Newtonian materialistic universe has been replaced by Quantum Physics; energy (nonmaterial reality – including thought and intelligence) – also known as "software" when consciously programmed – is part of our organic/biochemical "nature" – and we can feel its influence.

We can also begin to think of "chemistry" and "biology" in terms of software – and the Periodic Table of Elements as software "code" for how this "program" of Nature "operates.

In the following Periodic Table of Elements, some of these chemical elements when combined to form "molecules" are classified as "organic" – but what does this mean?

It simply means that a different level of programming is operational – higher conscious energies (or frequencies) are apparently at work.

This energy is what we call *life*.

Consciousness or Life "lives" through the manifestation and expression of various energies (perhaps some of them can be deemed intelligent) through these chemicals – which also comprise our DNA.

(Wikipedia describes the periodic table as a "tabular display" of the (known) chemical elements – if you compare it to the Genome, or "sequenced" DNA, it is just another set of symbols that help us comprehend Life and Nature – it is not Nature itself – it is "code" for Nature – or the basis for software).

If we add to this purely conceptual understanding of nature the fact that within "our" consciousness we have developed an artificial and basically arbitrary set of programs that we think of as "Me" we can begin to see how illusory our objective scientific view may be.

To the extent that materialistic science simply avoids the obvious reality of a conscious agency within nature (of which we are the prime example and of which we have firsthand experience) – our own conditioned adoption of this illusion creates much suffering.

Most important, and fortunately, this illusory operating system of a single, separate self apart from Nature/Life can be over ridden by a new layer of programming.

In the past we have called it mysticism, and we have sometimes attained it with psychedelics (different chemicals), which have temporarily suspended our programming (belief systems) to briefly glimpse outside Plato's cave.

No longer captives in the shadow, the result is a deeper connection with Life and a sense of "joy" – not the ephemeral "happiness" that the mass media promises through material gain, but an energetic connection that runs experientially deeper and that begins to soften the egoic sense of "Me".

This softened sense is less prone to anxiety and suffering because it begins to "trust Life" – it surrenders "control" because it begins to realize that "I am not in charge" – in fact, the deeper you look the more you will discover that "you" can "do" very little from the standpoint of a separate "I."

It is interesting to speculate where this separated sense of a fixed, solid "egoic" self came from. Is it the natural result of an evolved greater brain more able to survive through mental activity – as scientists would have us believe?

Or was there actually a "Fall of Man" – as the Bible and some religion suggests, or might that have been an actual bit of genetic "tampering" with our organism to increase suggestibility through our Ego – and more readily control our actions?

In his answer to what the "purpose" of this sometimes troublesome Ego – or collection of thoughts and belief systems – may be, Eckhart Tolle describes it beautifully as simply one natural part of the process of the intelligent evolution of Life.

Thought is part of what makes us human in much the same way as its scent makes the lily a flower. Through thought, however, our "self" becomes the key property of our mental existence just as Windows is a physical property and operating system of a computer.

I do not pretend to have the answer to how or why this reality came to be -- and in fact I think such contemplation is more profoundly effective when left as a deep QUESTION than allowing the mind to come up any number of facile answers.

The question seems to take to silence, and then deeper toward the truth – as Hofstadter suggests in *"I Am a Strange Loop"*.

As open questions these issues seem to activate deeper levels of software, in our brains and bodies that more directly connect us to Life and decrease our sense of separation and ultimately the fear of death.

If you have any doubt about how deeper levels of inner software can become activated – consider your favorite music.

"Lord my body has been a good friend
    But I won't need it when I reach the end"

– Cat Stevens: *Miles from Nowhere*

The Ego is instrumental (pun intended) in our survival. Its perpetual If/Then hypotheses may keep us from being eaten if we go into the jungle.

But of course this deeply conditioned software is energized by fear of death.

Eckhart Tolle says, the opposite of death is not life, but birth. In this context both birth and its opposite (death) are natural processes within a supreme intelligence (Life/Consciousness/God); within this cosmology the Ego which fears the body's demise as its own, is phantom.

But it is precisely this deeply sensed fear of the extinguishing of our sensory and mental processes that increases the potential for external control – by others and today by the mass media – through the fear of violence (terrorism) or sense of lack (not measuring up to society's standards).

In this way our inner software becomes subject to inputs that are actually harmful to our mental and emotional state.

It is hardly surprising that it is precisely our inner programming that puts us to "sleep" and makes us susceptible to mass delusion and false belief systems.

These programs that act upon our false beliefs are in fact the powerful reactive "negative emotions" Gurdjieff describes in his teaching which keep us trapped in a state of unconsciousness or sleep. Gurdjieff/Ouspensky groups employ various techniques including self-observation, contemplation, and even dance and movements that (in modern terms) may help in reprogramming our three brains (harmonious consciousness) and reconnect us with Life (higher centers).

But as many of us have experienced, living without awareness of how our conditioned behavior patterns make us perceive reality, and shape our experience, can lead to despair, and a sense of powerlessness. We see ourselves perpetually as victims of circumstances.

As my friend Michael Jeffreys says, "Don't be a victim [under outside control] – become a 'scientist' and actually experiment with these energies."

Simply noticing how we function, as opposed to our imagination of how we think we function, or worse **how we think we should** function, can open many new doors.

You can begin to see many of the same results with meditation and yoga as you do with better nutrition and self-observation.

Such conscious practices are actually forming new software programs and begin to overwrite the "grooved" belief systems unconsciously stored in our DNA and brains.

Like a new computer operating system –in greater alignment with the ebb and flow of Life – truly higher energies can eventually lead to a lessening of separation and an increase in vitality.

And of course the word "vitality" is based on "vi" – which is the Latin root for Life itself.

All of this begins to crystallize when we see ourselves as operating non-materially – no longer operating within a purely mechanical Newtonian universe – but as the energetic expression of an immense intelligence. In other words … Software.

2.9

What About God?

Of course as noted previously, we have traditionally given a name or label to this sense of higher intelligence or mystery in a religious context. Some of us worship this concept as "God".

When today's well-known atheists ridicule the Gods of organized religion they are really going after the low hanging fruit. It is easy to logically "disprove" or question the existence of a God "created in our own image" – the vengeful anthropomorphic Guy with a beard who is at the same time omnipotent and allows suffering and war.

"The machine code of the genes is uncannily computer-like"

--Richard Dawkins, *River Out of Eden*, (1995).

Atheists like Richard Dawkins, Stephen Hawking and Bill Maher love to point out the obvious flaws in the low hanging fruit: Fundamentalism and Creationism which take scripture literally and not mythically.

But this is not the only way to approach the great mystery that sometimes fills the "variable" we call God with conceptual beliefs, based on literal interpretation of ancient texts and stories.

We need to remember that there are also western traditions of Pantheism and Deism that echo the wisdom teachings of Native Americans, who held the land sacred and did not believe it could be "owned".

Most of our own "founding fathers" were in fact Deists – not conventional Christians. Deists also included the American transcendentalists like Emerson, Whitman and Thoreau.

And there have been cultures that seem to have had a sacred science more aligned with nature that we know only from their fragmentary remains. From their hieroglyphs we know that the Egyptians worshipped intelligent natural forces call "Neters". Neters would include the cyclical flooding of the Nile that irrigated their crops.

Recall also that the Egyptians encoded the mathematical constant Pi in the Great Pyramid – the relationship between the radius of a circle and its circumference was deemed fundamental to the Cosmos ad sacred.

In addition to Pi, the Egyptians also encoded the constant Phi – the sacred relationship in which each subsequent number is the sum of the previous two integers – also known today as the Fibonacci sequence and found everywhere in nature.

These mathematical constants represented the perfect forms of Geometry revered by Plato, and might also comprise the fragmentary remnants of a sacred science from an even older lost civilization.

It is interesting to consider that another Greek mathematician; Pythagoras attributed much of his knowledge to Egyptian culture. It is tragic to consider the massive ancient wisdom that was probably consumed in the fire of the Library of Alexandria.

It is important here to bear in mind that for the Greeks, and presumably for the Egyptians who enshrined mathematical constants in their monuments, that Geometry was not a purely theoretical reflection of the Deity.

"Mathematics is the alphabet with which God has written the universe."

– Galileo Galilei

2.10

Must the "Programmer" be a "Who"?

A resurgence of Greek and Egyptian mathematics and Geometry appeared during the Italian Renaissance.

Phi was known as the "Golden Mean" during the Renaissance and also memorialized in the great works of Leonardo da Vinci.

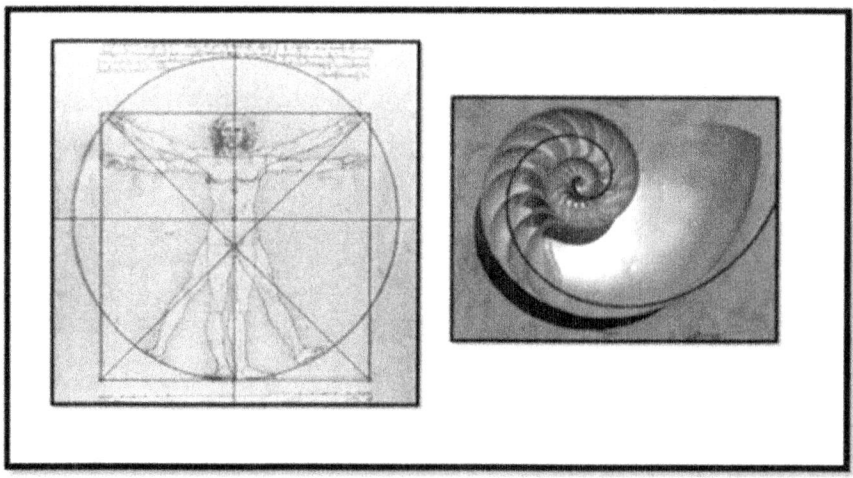

The Fibonacci sequence, in which each number is the sum of the previous two, can be represented as a triangle in two dimensions, or as a pyramid in three.

If DNA is Software, Who Wrote the Code?   By Tom Bunzel

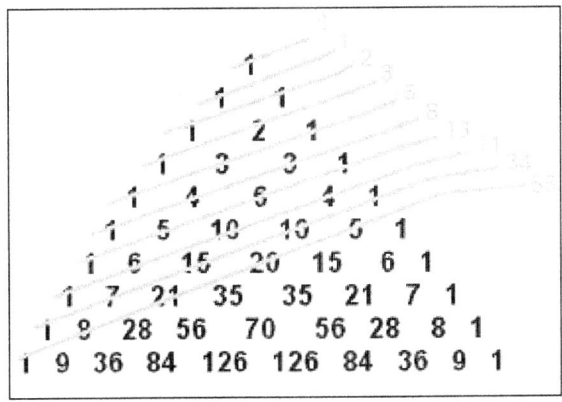

– http://www.mathacademy.com/pr/prime/articles/fibonac/fibonac_9.gif

I have long been fascinated by math but I reached a precipice in school when I ran up against calculus; I once asked my teacher if he could explain by example what in nature represents "the function of a number" – I was desperate, I said, because I could see the application of Geometry and algebra, in which I excelled, but not calculus.

He looked at me disdainfully and said simply, "no." That's when I switched to Liberal Arts.

Ironically, my current fascination with computers is the result of their "living" functions – software – which are mathematical algorithms that perform tasks – they are active verbs – and contradict many of the assumptions of today's materialist science.

In "*I Am a Strange Loop*," Douglas R. Hofstadter's follow-up to a Pulitzer prize winning best-seller, Gödel, Escher, Bach: An Eternal Golden Braid demonstrates the unique qualities of a mind that expresses itself in language, along with the inevitable gaps and paradoxes that result in believing too much in the logic of our spoken and written descriptions of "what is real".

He explores the mental and perhaps "quantum" gap between language or words – the programming of the "Ego" – and mathematics – what Galileo and others have considered the language of God.

As a mathematician, neuroscientist and philosopher Hofstadter begins with the primacy of number because whatever symbols you use to represent "number", certain truths persist.

That would be why the ancients considered these spatial relationships sacred.

For example, as Pythagoras famously asserted, the sums of the squares of a right triangle always add up to the square of the hypotenuse.

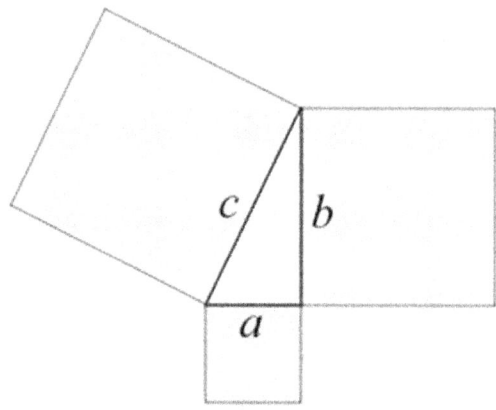

Remember – and consider – it does not matter what you call these "concepts" – the relationships they represent in physical space always hold true.

Hofstadter, like Leonardo da Vinci, focuses on this famous series of numbers that are also manifest in nature, and to many throughout history have represented a Golden Mean, Golden Ratio or Perfect Ratio, also called the number Phi (not Pi).

If DNA is Software, Who Wrote the Code? By Tom Bunzel

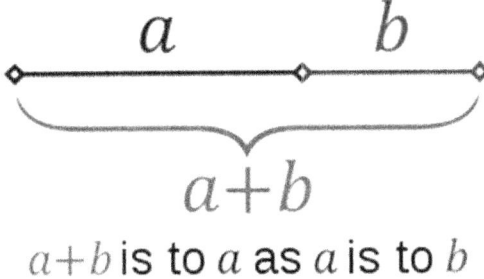

$a+b$ is to a as a is to b

— "Prime Number." Wikipedia. Wikimedia Foundation. Web. 23 May 2016. <https://en.wikipedia.org/wiki/Prime_number>.

In mathematics, the Fibonacci numbers are the numbers that conform to this ratio in the following sequence of integers:

0, 1, 1, 2, 3, 5, 8, 13, 21, 34, 55, 89, 144, 233, 377, 610, 987, 1597, 2584, 4181, 6765, 10946, 17711, 28657, 46368, 75025, 121393, 196418, 317811

By definition, the first two numbers in the Fibonacci sequence are 0 and 1, and each subsequent number is the sum of the previous two, (in the relation of Phi= 1.61803399).

If I understand Hofstadter's key point, it is that the idea that lies behind such a **significant** sequence of numbers is primary and causal – and can be described in a different set of symbols, namely the English language as – "a sequence of numbers such that each subsequent number is the sum of the previous two".

Similarly one can define some members of this "set" of numbers in English as being "prime", that is, indivisible by any number other than themselves and the number 1.

One can come up with very complex theorems and formulae to "describe" the relationships to ascertain which numbers, as one gets very large approaching infinity, are in fact prime and members of the Fibonacci sequence.

What Hofstadter points out, however, is the discovery of mathematician Kurt Gödel, that when one goes from the primary set of symbols (numbers) to our "understanding" of them represented by language; i.e., though about those symbols, very weird anomalies of logic come up that result in "*I Am a Strange Loop*" – infinite progressions without resolution.

In terms of scale, it is interesting to consider that there are vast Prime Numbers whose characteristics we can describe (indivisible by any number other than themselves and the number 1), and yet which our own brains and even the supercomputers we've invented have not yet "discovered" – yet which according to our language, analogies and suppositions must exist …

It was proven by Euclid that there are infinitely many Prime Numbers; thus, there is always a prime greater than the largest known prime.

– "Prime Number." Wikipedia. Wikimedia Foundation. Web. 23 May 2016. <https://en.wikipedia.org/wiki/Prime_number>.

Here is an example of another such paradox or anomaly:
"The sentence 'This sentence has ten words', has ten words." (*I Am a Strange Loop*)

Here we can see how our verbal or linguistic description of a mathematical truth (which is absolute – see the infallibility of the Fibonacci sequence stretching out to infinity) is inevitably fraught with fallacy and "looping". This strikes me as significant to several levels. First if we look at how we use computer software to manifest concepts through software, we first write them out in code (language) and then compile them into a sequence of numbers (zeros and ones) to express in "reality" (through the physical machine) – displaying on screen and interacting with other users.

To Hofstadter (I think), this paradoxical aspect of **language is an obvious manifestation of Mind which simulates nature on a very powerful level** – by analogy it seems to mirror our own inner mental workings – but it cannot "explain" nature or for that matter infinite sequences of number. It can only explain characteristics.

Language, like our inner "I", is looped and imperfect – with the inherent limitation of needing to be expressed in words, and consequently reducing the perfection of the absolute it describes (mathematical certainly; number) to what our limited minds can comprehend – fragmented, imperfect analogies to reality.

But in its perfection as "Form" mathematics and specifically Geometry, for the Greeks, suggested an immensely intelligent (perfect) mental component to reality.

2.11

Nature as Geometry

In *I Am a Strange Loop*, Hofstadter also takes issue with futurists like Ray Kurzweil who believe that our artificial intelligence will naturally evolve according to Moore's law and inexorably lead to a conscious (Turing) machine with fully natural (human) qualities, indistinguishable from another (real) person.

To me the inevitable fallacy of any concept of a "living" artificial intelligence comes as the result of realizing that in nature this "software" (true Consciousness or Being) represents a scale of intelligence far beyond our own.

This difference in scale is precisely the gap between the understanding possible in language (or symbolic truth) and mathematics/Geometry (perfection or infinite Intelligence).

As an example, in nature, our limited conception of the universe is as "infinite." We also know that a sequence of numbers is "infinite" and yet the largest actual numbers are still inaccessible to our limited minds – and even our supercomputers.

Similarly, when looking up at the heavens, the word "infinite" comes to mind, but the reality is much more stark and real and far beyond any mental comprehension. In fact, within this experience, it is frequently felt in "all three brains" (Gurdjieff) – in the gut and in the heart – as a connection to a truth that exists in a dimension beyond space and time (which are again mental constructs).

Just as thought makes pure Consciousness appear as time, so perception makes pure Consciousness appear as space.

– Rupert Spira

On the other hand, within nature the Fibonacci sequence manifests imperfectly but potentially infinitely in living forms:

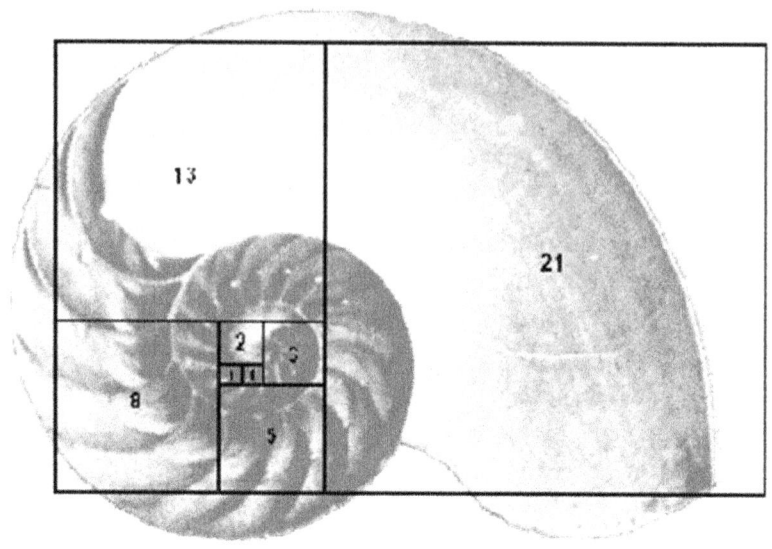

– http://www.mathacademy.com/pr/prime/articles/fibonac/fibonac_8.gif

And as a species, evolving as we have to make advances, a field called **Biomimicry** has emerged – biologically inspired engineering; other examples include Sharkskin inspired swimsuit – that pay homage to the higher perfection of Life or Nature in its manifestation of Number in Form (Matter).

One might well argue that computer software itself – created in "our image" – is an example of inadvertent biomimicry of our mental functions.

Then sequencing DNA becomes a matter of actually decoding how these intentional instructions from a higher Mind operate – and the supercomputers become yet another example of unconscious biomimicry.

If we also consider the explosive nature of Moore's Law – where the processing power of the chips that process computer data was to double every two years – we can see another example of biomimicry in action; that is, the means of accomplishing this is making the electronics smaller and smaller, and more and more "life-like."

In fact this area is expanding into Nano computing and the use of ever smaller and more sophisticated sensors and other devices that mimic more and more of Life's intelligence.

The problem, of course, continue to be our identification with the thinking processes what we take for granted but which can be exposed as inadequate to the task of truly comprehending nature.

We can see this again, clearly, in mathematics.

Hofstadter deconstructs the famed mathematician Gödel's work to basically argue that the only way to comprehend consciousness is through "story" – or by analogy – and just as the linguistic descriptions of mathematical absolutes fall short, so too does story or analogy; which can never completely "explain" or "describe" the true "nature" of consciousness.

Ultimately he settles on one aspect of language as the pointer to reality and meaning – *analogy*; so keep in mind our issue with the "metaphor" of software.

In reality, Life operates as software with exquisite perfection, unlike the computer code which we have written "in its image" and which frequently crashes.

Hofstadter's sense of what is "animate" comes down to the existence of the self-sustaining loops that will literally "blow our minds" – like the placement of two mirrors facing each other or his example of a video feedback loop of a camera facing a monitor.

He writes, "… an entity is animate [alive?] to the *degree* that such a loopy 'I' pattern comes into existence, since this pattern's existence is by no means an all-or-nothing affair. Thus, to the extent that there is an "I" pattern in a given substrate, there is animacy, and where there is no such pattern, the entity is inanimate."

Hofstadter's contends that as systems evolved, for example cells organized into organs like the heart and eventually the brain, when feedback loops manifest as "selves" – at this point organic molecules become animate or "alive".

This resonates perfectly with the evolutionary perspective of Eckhart Tolle with respect to the Ego; when this "sacred" feedback loop evolved as the software of the brain the organism equated the concept of the self with its frenetic mental activity.

Language and writing, and now media have served to solidify the apparent reality of the Ego. That delusion is hopefully coming to an end.

Hofstadter still assumes, however, that such organization happened by evolution randomly, even if according to nature's patterns such as the Fibonacci sequence.

But I see it another way. I find the very existence of such patterns evidence of the presence of a quality in nature that science finds "unscientific" but which I consider the "presence of mind".

Mind is a higher level or function of order and indeed mathematics (Function=another pun) – and our ignorance of that in our current culture is the root of many problems. Philosopher Jacob Needleman refers to this delusion as "Scientism" in books such as *A Sense of the Cosmos*.

Indeed the march of science has now even illuminated the fact that all of nature conforms to such patterns – the subject of an enormous book by James Gleick, *The Information*, which essentially traces the human discovery of meaning within nature according to what science considers "data".

But remember the key premise – there can be no such "thing" as data without Mind. Data is order discerned from chaos based on a system of consistency; all of which must be within the domain of Mind.

Who or what is there to discern order without Mind?

If we can then open slightly to the possibility, beyond our intellect or conditioning, and consider that perhaps Life is more than mere data – that the animate force behind life (which the Egyptians thought of as the function Phi – the mathematical ratio of the Fibonacci sequence) *literally* – is Mind – an immaterial intelligence of which we are mainly ignorant – a great deal suddenly begins to actually make "sense" in a different way.

Consider the fact that the Pythagorean Theorem and the Fibonacci sequence did not originate with the Greeks, its knowledge is far more ancient and was considered *sacred* by ancient civilizations, such as the Egyptians.

As I have noted, in addition to the Pi relationship, the Phi relationship and the Pythagorean relationship of the sides of the right triangle are apparently depicted in ancient monoliths – and the starkest and famous example is the Great Pyramid of Giza.

I became fascinated with this concept when I first read *Secrets of the Great Pyramid: Two Thousand Years of Adventures and Discoveries Surrounding the Mysteries of the Great Pyramid of Cheops,* by Peter Tompkins, which incidentally has an appendix by a renowned Italian mathematician, Livio Stecchini that further probes the depths of these relationships.

The key point here is that the ancient wisdom did not distinguish between science and religion – the awareness of this higher nature of Life as the manifestation of an infinite Mind was sacred – as were many of the rituals that were meant to preserve this knowledge.

Of course, in the vast spans of time since this knowledge was fully flourishing, we are left with mere fragments that are further distorted and ignored by conventional archeology and astronomy – our science is cut off entirely from the fields of religion and philosophy.

And we can only speculate where this ancient wisdom originated. For those of you with open minds (and fertile imaginations), I recommend the Ancient Aliens series on the History Channel and the work of Erik von Daniken, and more recently the discoveries of Graham Hancock, author of *Magicians of the Gods: The Forgotten Wisdom of Earth's Lost Civilization.*

But what ties all of this together is the Platonic notion of a conceptual form or idea behind the truth of Life itself as it expresses through mathematical perfection.

The participation or primacy of a "personal" entity is no longer required at the heart of nature. It simply unfolds according to law. This notion is shared even by fervent atheists like Stephen Hawking, although their sense of awe and more important a sacred reverence as the proper attitude in response to this discovery continues to be lacking.

2.12

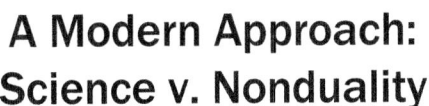

A Modern Approach: Science v. Nonduality

It is interesting to ponder, as our own science, both in the area of quantum physics and neuroscience, comes up against the barrier of "who" is knowing, the pantheistic beliefs of one of our own greatest scientists.

"Common to all these types is the anthropomorphic character of their conception of God. In general, only individuals of exceptional endowments, and exceptionally high-minded communities, rise to any considerable extent above this level. But there is a third stage of religious experience which belongs to all of them, even though it is rarely found in a pure form: **I shall call it cosmic religious feeling.** It is very difficult to elucidate this feeling to anyone who is entirely without it, especially as there is no anthropomorphic conception of God corresponding to it."

– Albert Einstein: *The World As I See It*

This "cosmic religious feeling" was shared by other physicists of Einstein's time along with the great mystics of the east. It was also part of the belief system of the Deists – the "founding fathers" who authored our own Declaration of Independence and Constitution, and the Transcendentalists: Whitman, Emerson and Thoreau.

Today our own scientific instruments have extended our human sensory capacity exponentially, and yet at each turn we discover energies and influences that are beyond our normal range of sight, hearing or any other capacity to discern.

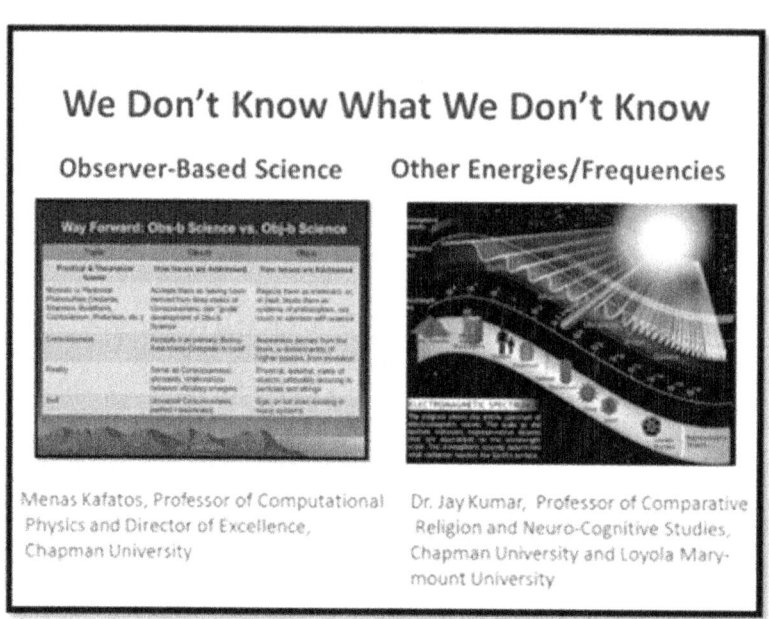

These are the subject areas of conferences like Science and Nonduality and Wisdom 2.0.

At the Science and Nonduality Conference there is an ongoing attempt to merge the scientific disciplines of neuroscience and physics with an empirical understanding of the nature of consciousness itself, but it is difficult because as some have noted (Rupert Spira), science is by its nature dualistic – positing a subject and object.

The subject is the scientist – the world is viewed as an objective entity that seems to pause long enough to be understood "scientifically." But of course in reality, there is never a pause to Life and no actual separation between subject and object.

Other movements by respected scientists have attempted to reconcile the reality of our biological existence with what can reasonably be known – to develop a science of Being.

Previously mentioned, biologist Dr. Robert Lanza, whose work is in stem cell research, has coined the phrase "Biocentrism" to attempt to understand our unique perspective based upon our biological ontology (being).

Biocentrism

"There is nothing in modern physics that explains how a group of molecules in a brain creates consciousness. The beauty of a sunset, the taste of a delicious meal, these are all mysteries to science — which can sometimes pin down where in the brain the sensations arise, but not how and why there is any subjective personal experience to begin with.

And, what's worse, nothing in science can explain how consciousness arose from matter. Our understanding of this most basic phenomenon is virtually nil. *Interestingly, most models of physics do not even recognize this as a problem*."

http://www.robertlanza.com/biocentrism-how-life-creates-the-universe/

Biocentrism is a new "theory of biological relativity", rethinking our view of reality relative to our biology – and finally inclusive of consciousness. According to Dr. Robert Lanza and Robert Berman the authors of *Biocentrism: How Life Creates the Universe*. Life (or Consciousness) is primary, not the accidental occurrence of a random and lifeless universe.

Our biology therefore is the default basis for our notion of reality, and our experience (which science has not accounted for) include a Consciousness that seems to exist outside of Space/Time – an infinite intelligence.

All of these movements seem to be echoing another area of the new genetics called "Epigenetics" and heralded by Bruce Lipton in his classic: *The Biology of Belief*.

More recently Deepak Chopra and Dr. Rudy Tanzi have addressed this reality – that the genes or our DNA are not determinative but rather aspects of an entire natural relationship between our "selves" and our genes, our skin, and the environment – again, Epigenetics.

Super Genes: Unlock the Astonishing Power of Your DNA for Optimum Health and Well-Being by Deepak Chopra M.D. and Rudolph E. Tanzi was published as I write this. (Dr. Rudolph Tanzi is a renowned neuroscientist specializing in Alzheimer's).

While Deepak Chopra has always been a thought leader in the area of how the mind/body functions from a non-materialist perspective, in this book Chopra and co-author Dr. Tanzi address the latest field of science – biophysics and Epigenetics.

When DNA was first discovered, it was thought that it was a deterministic part of our cells, which unilaterally was responsible for various functions, and conditions and diseases. However the more recent findings in "Epigenetics" have discovered that DNA actually works in harmony with the environment, and through the skin membrane and brain, in an interactive way.

"You are not simply the sum total of the genes you were born with." write Deepak Chopra and Rudy Tanzi. "You are the user and controller of your genes, the author of your biological story. No prospect in self-care is more exciting."

Bruce Lipton, posted the following in his review of Chopra and Tanzi's work:

"Once thought to be the domain of genes, the control of health and behavior is now dynamically linked to the environment, and more importantly, our perception of the environment ... Drs. Chopra and Tanzi's contribution is a valuable resource that empowers us to become the masters of our fate rather than the 'victims' of our heredity."

Dr. Tanzi's research into Alzheimer's suggests that the "Self" is a core belief system (operating system?) that becomes damaged or malfunctioning during this debilitating disease. This finding goes to the likelihood that our identities are not static or set in stone, but rather evolve and change fluidly.

Of course the foundation of the self are its stored memories – which are inaccessible when this horrible disease is contracted.

In fact other researchers like David Eagleman and Joe Dispenza have written about how the neuroplasticity of the brain allows it to constantly adapt and change – to learn new behaviors and to take on different personalities, also in harmony with the environment.

I got a brief taste of its breadth and scope at this year's Science and Nonduality Conference where Deepak Chopra said that Wikipedia has at least 15-20 current "explanations" of quantum mechanics, "Nobody knows what's going on. The math works but no one knows … **Your body is a metaphor for experiencing reality."**

1. What's universe made of? (We don't know.)
2. What is the biological basis of consciousness? (We have no answer.)

According to Deepak there is simply no explanation for perceptional/mental experience or "qualia" without somehow addressing the question: *"Who is having experience?"* – which is precisely the question he poses to conventional scientists that inevitably brings them to what Deepak said was simply a "dead end."

In science this is referred to as "… *the hard problem of consciousness".*

He asks, "Where is the I?" The reality is that the "I center" of experience cannot be found. Deepak says, echoing Rupert Spira with whom he shared the stage at SAND, that consciousness has "no dimension."
And how does science "explain" the biggest mystery of all?

2.13

Life Happened How?

While ridiculing the fundamentalist religions in their ascribing the beginning of life to a "God" it is instructive to take a closer look now at how our science addresses the issue. The following graphics are from a NASA video about biology.

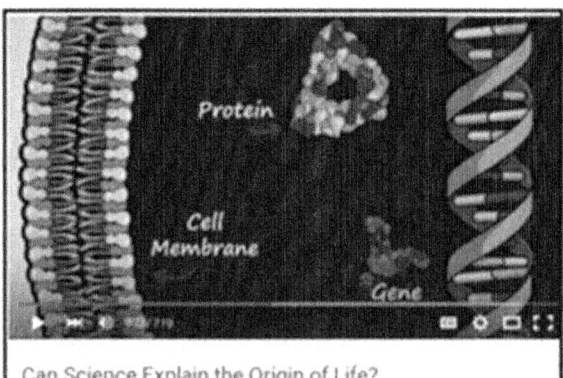

– "Homepage | The Center for Chemical Evolution." Homepage | The Center for Chemical Evolution. Web. 23 May 2016.

The NASA video goes through a "reasonable" description of what we know about our own cells and identifies the genes and DNA.

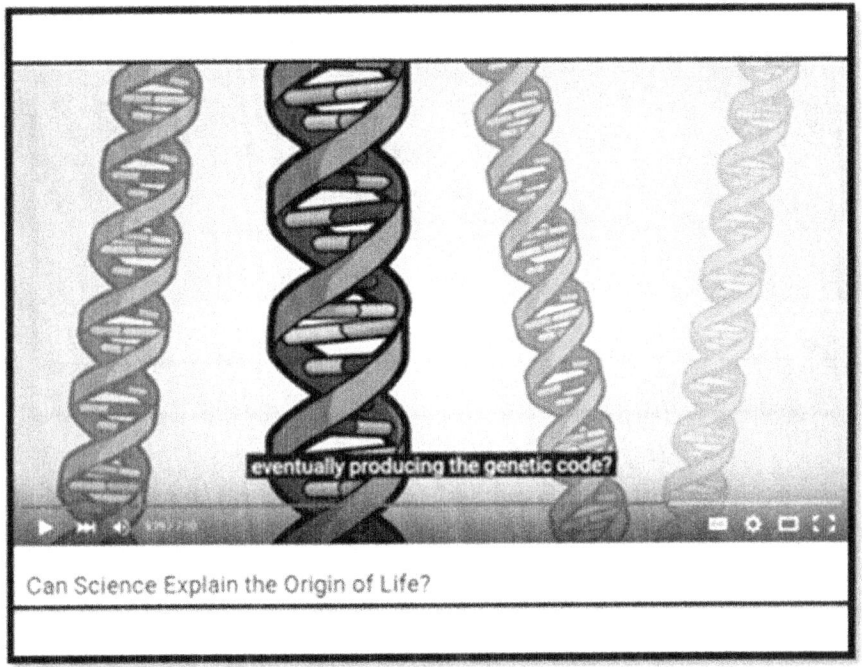

But it never really gets into "HOW" this genetic code might have originated and begun the process of evolving into higher life forms.

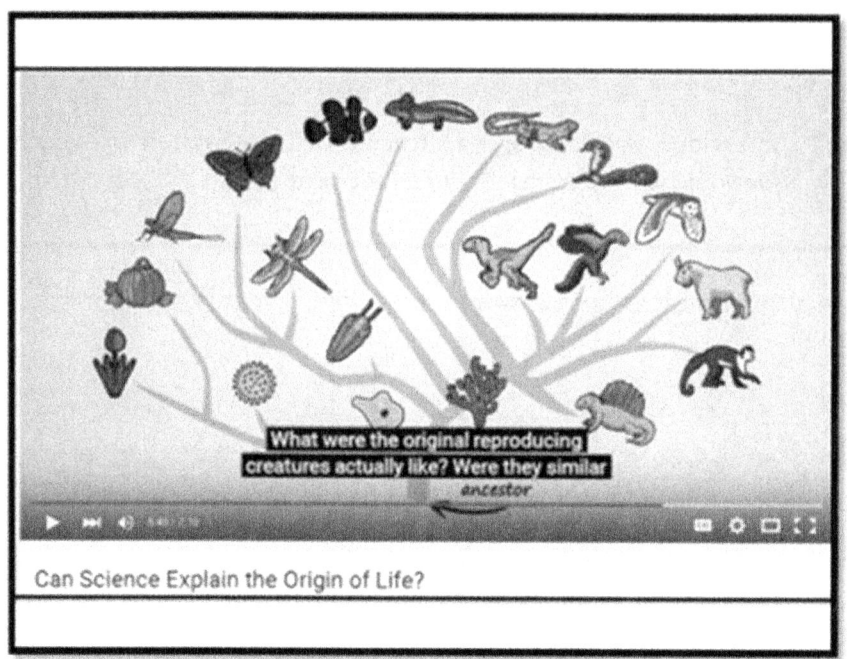

It conveniently skirts this issue and does not leave it open, but rather suggests that there may be an explanation. At the same time it does what science does best – it labels the "properties" and different expressions of life very well (above).

There's a nice graphic with an arrow of how organic compounds "sprung to life" but absolutely no account of how those chemicals are able to have experiences (or the basis for qualia), as Deepak Chopra and others point out.

And to reiterate what Dr. Robert Lanza says, there is no explanation for how something material can become conscious – which is another way of saying – has experience.

And once there is an "outside force" it must be accounted for as well.

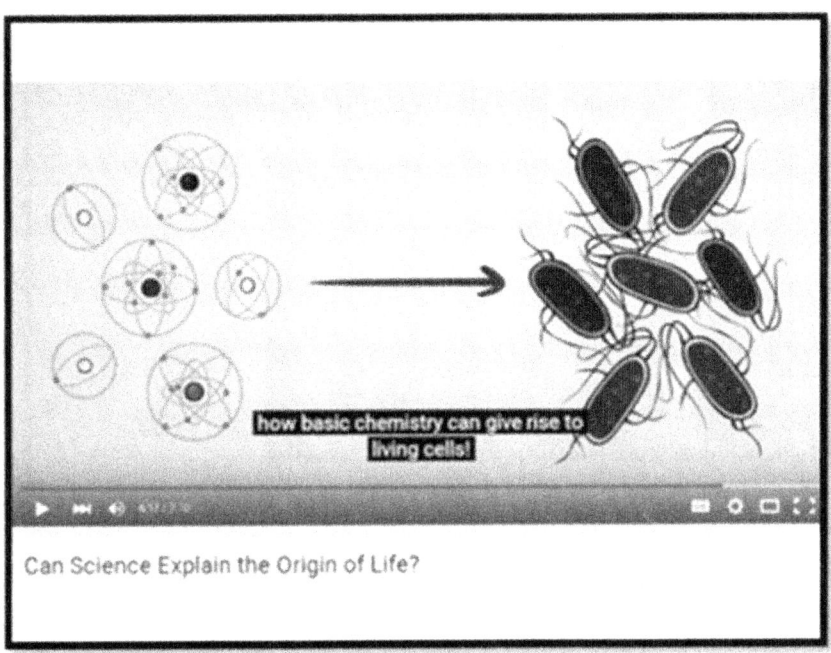

The obvious question is: How can inanimate matter be or become conscious?

NASA and the rest of conventional science have no answer for this very inconvenient question.

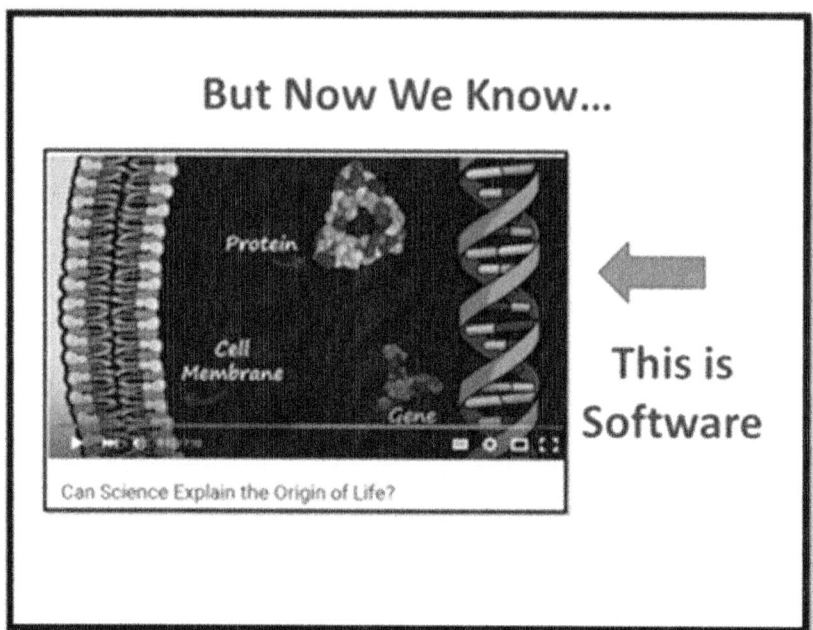

However, in my view, thanks to the leaps in computer science we now have an apt description for a nonmaterial active intelligence, which can be encoded in organic matter – or silicon.

We call it software.

This changes everything.

As we have seen in detail, the operation of DNA is now actually known to us through another science – computer science.

The inner working of DNA is completely logical and according to syntax. **We have identified it as an organic programming language.**

This recognition brings up the view of another noted scientist, astronomer and physicist Fred Hoyle, as to the possible "accidental" arising of life – and DNA.

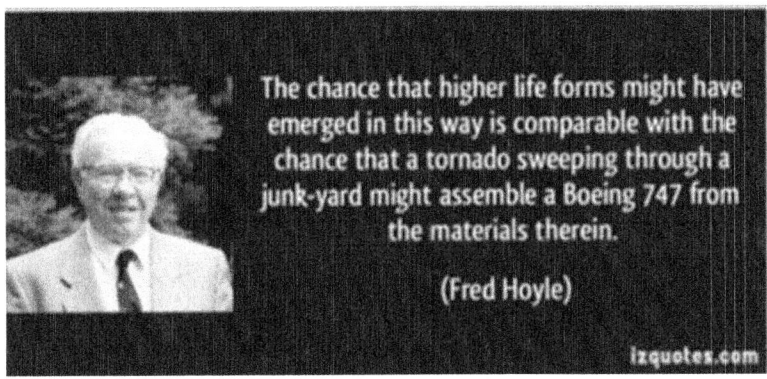

If we honestly address the discoveries we have made there is only one conclusion that is possible, without the shortcut of referring to a God or some other supernatural theory.

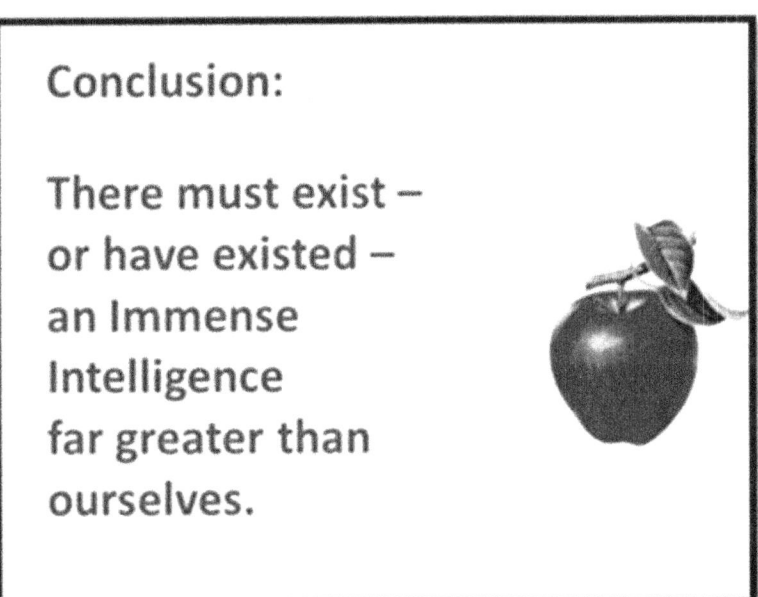

Part 3.0

A Shift in My Programming
Truth and Consequences

Confronting the reality that what we are, is based on a complex biological programming language that predates us, and that is obvious the product of an immense intelligence, is not always comfortable.

After all, science itself deals with what is knowable. Discovering the limitations of our deepest held beliefs could be disconcerting. When the "doors of perception" abruptly open and we begin to recognize the glaring omissions in the scientific worldview, we can be left with many more questions – and a deep void – wondering who and what we are.

But at least we are no longer harboring the delusion that we know things that we do not.

I have already alluded to some of the ramifications of dropping many of our most accepted beliefs – including a complete rethinking of human history and questioning the materialist tenets of modern science.

In his book *The Four Agreements*, Don Miguel Ruiz refers to our belief systems, or the conditioned "truths" we take as given through our parents, teachers and peers, as dreams.

The Four Agreements is based on Toltec wisdom and comes to us as an oral teaching. But in the context of our discussion in modern terms, we can really call these agreements our "programming".

The scientific and technological aspects of reality led me back to where I originally began my search for "answers" as a young man, but then when I revisited those experiences as T.S. Eliot famously wrote I, "saw them again for the very first time".

3.1

Rediscovering Ancient Wisdom

While the epiphany that led to this book began in 2007, my real suspicions about the subject matter began when I was about 25, working as a tour director in Cancun, Mexico. There I visited the ruins of Chichen Itza and was struck by the similarity in structure of the monuments and language of the Maya (the name for these people is the same as the word for illusion in Sanskrit).

And of course they built pyramids, as did the Aztecs. And in the greatest of ironies it was in the Yucatan that a young friend, a bellman at the hotel, gave me a book by a Mexican archeologist about those other pyramids. He gave me *Dramatic Prophecies of the Great Pyramid* by Rudolfo Benavides.

This led me to two more "credible" books by the author of the best-seller, "*The Secret Life of Plants*," Peter Tompkins – his lesser known works: *Secrets of the Great Pyramid* and *Secrets of the Mayan Pyramid*.

Beginning to suspect that much of what I had been taught in school was incomplete at best, I continued to seek answers to questions modern science sees as irrelevant.

This search led me to another teaching of a sage who appeared in Russia at the beginning of the 20th century, and who spent years working at the Great Pyramid and claimed to have gleaned some of its secrets: G. I. Gurdjieff.

Gurdjieff's work was the subject of *In Search of the Miraculous* by one of his students, Peter D. Ouspensky and has been the subject of controversy because "schools" that still exist dedicated to his psychological beliefs and cosmology are sometimes derided as cults.

I never stayed in any of these groups but read the material over the years and as computer science emerged, it became clear to me that Gurdjieff, along with his contemporary Nicolai Tesla, had some sort of connection with, and truly understood, significant aspects of ancient wisdom.

Gurdjieff cryptically referred to a map of "pre-sand" Egypt that informed his early studies, and when asked about the source for his system he said it was "pre-Christianity" – from a version of Christianity that was before Egypt and profoundly influenced all subsequent human thought.

This notion of a source of ancient wisdom intrigued me, and it began my interest in the work of one of Gurdjieff's most famous modern students, philosopher Jacob Needleman who wrote *Lost Christianity*.

This alternative view of the story of Jesus, as a great teacher of ancient wisdom, fascinated me because this new perspective suggested connection to a higher intelligence that was impersonal (not anthropomorphic) and the source of all Being. Even more significant was that this "ancient Christianity" echoed so profoundly the teachings of Eastern religions like Buddhism and Hinduism and its source was in the remote past – before even dynastic Egypt.

As I read further it became clearer and clearer that the Gnostics, who faithfully continued this lost traditional teaching (that was later distorted and politicized by the Church), had a fascinating view of sin: **the Gnostics viewed sin <u>psychologically</u> as the mind's resistance to what is.**

And more recently, when I began reading the work of Eckhart Tolle, who also provides re-interpretations of the parables of Jesus, all of this began to make sense on a physical and emotional – and not merely intellectual level.

The Gnostics (and Gurdjieff/Ouspensky), Eckhart Tolle and the Eastern mystics, and the modern neuroscientists and quantum physicists all had several things in common:

- They all view the "monkey-mind" * – the voice in the head – as the source of suffering.
- (For those steeped in "Scientism," this suffering entails an inability to find certainty within a material model of reality).
- Human suffering derives from a belief in how things should be, rather than how things ARE – the fruit of the tree of the knowledge of Good and Evil (Duality) was the mistaken belief that the voice in the head is who we are.
- Listening to this voice led to disharmony and the existence of numerous "I"s or "centers" within the self.
- There is no "one core self" – and understanding this takes one beyond the beliefs of the inner monkey-mind and to, as Eckhart Tolle explains, the true "Kingdom of Heaven" – which is of course to be found **not** in the external world of "things" but rather within – in connection with the immense intelligence of Life itself.

Gurdjieff had referred to his teaching as "The Fourth Way," beyond the traditional esoteric paths of the asceticism, mysticism or deprivation, and to be accomplished directly within the tests and circumstances of the modern world.

His aim was to bring together the wisdom of the East and West, and to address the one key question: **"What is the sense and significance of life on earth, and human life in particular."**

Put another way, this question is also the basis of modern Epigenetics, neuroscience, quantum physics and biocentrism: to recognize the limitations of the materialist worldview and to put our science back into alignment with the immense intelligence which we sense that we are when we harmonize all aspects of our being.

Epigenetics, quantum physics and modern neuroscience have one thing in common – they all see scientific truth as reflected in the interconnected systems – the networks – of the natural universe – and their continued activity which never pauses …

A new science will study reality as a verb – as opposed to labeling separate "silos" of nouns within disparate disciplines like biology, physics, geology etc.

For example as noted previously, Epigenetics has recently gained traction in biology as the study of the role of genes within an interconnected environment, in which humans play an important role, but of which we are neither the masters nor the creators.

Using the concept of Epigenetics as the pointer to a possible follow-up to Gurdjieff's question, we might now begin to speculate that all organic life, and human life in particular, **has the function of transmuting the highly intelligent (and as yet unknown) energies of the universe in the service of evolution – the creation of (intelligent) order from chaos.**

But this is a highly conceptual answer. The reality is not conceptual after all – it is manifest only within the lived experience of those who come upon this level of potential truth – and those experiences are not always pleasant.

The generally imagined outcome of "enlightenment" is that suddenly the clouds part, music plays, and we live in continual heavenly bliss.

However if there even is such a thing as awakening, the reality is far different. It involves a practical commitment to actual experience and truth within the only thing that is known for sure – the certainty of "I am" – existence itself. This all-important truth can only ever be directly encountered in the present moment.

* The term "Monkey-Mind" comes from the image of the monkey, swinging from overhead limb to overhead limb, grasping and releasing each new branch as he travels through the trees. Similarly, we grasp and release each new thought the mind creates for us as we travel through life.

3.2

Journey to a New Operating System

The problem with the dawning of this recognition that "something is off" is that it immediately puts one at odds with many established belief systems, and challenges many of the assumptions upon which we build our lives.

In my case, as I became aware that there might be "more than one of me" and I noticed this, it was disconcerting.

More than ever, my sense of separation from everything and everyone else was palpable. The voices in my head clamored for answers and offered many contradictory explanations and courses of action, all of which exhausted me.

Most people with whom I spoke had no comprehension of these ideas and lived a reality that I no longer accepted or understood – chasing ideals and goals that I now found largely meaningless.

The people who did seem to understand some of what I had come to believe or intuit seemed even stranger. Many of them believed I had to join groups, read more books, sit cross-legged, learn ancient dances, or otherwise drop many of the things I took as "normal".

And then in 2008, I suddenly lost several sources of income; I also ended a relationship, and as the economy unraveled I came to fear what I had begun to suspect on September 11, 2001: that we were going to enter a new dark age very much like what my parents had experienced in Europe during World War II.

I no longer knew what to believe or who I was, and I had a breakdown. Of course I later learned as I read Eckhart Tolle's work that he had had a similar breakdown when he "could not stand himself".

3.3

Surrender

The bottom fell out for me at the tennis court. I have been an avid player for many years and often practiced against the wall. Suddenly, with my beliefs and bearings threatened, I "forgot" how to hit a forehand.

I remember trying to begin to hit a ball at the wall, trying to set up for a forehand, and flailing it not to the top of the wall, but over a fence that extended another 15 feet higher.

I later learned from my therapist that there was a neurological component to my sudden loss of muscle memory, but in the context of all that I was experiencing, I was completely lost.

My mind reeled. Stories circulated through my head about strokes, aneurisms and any other worst-case scenario and I found myself sobbing for no reason.

I was also tired all the time. I could barely get up in the morning and make myself breakfast and the only time I felt at peace was under the comforter on my bed.

I tried desperately to find answers. I tried homeopathic remedies and stereophonic music to try to sleep at night, when I tossed and turned for hours. I had shooting currents up and down my arms and legs – panic attacks.

My doctor prescribed tranquilizers, which helped for brief periods, but he could find no other physical symptoms.

I tried to work and go out and participate in life but I felt separate from everything else. I was beyond lethargy; I realized I was out of control.

As I lay under the covers I told myself the rest of the world could go on without me. I had to somehow get through this but for the moment, there was nothing left to try, to do or to plan.

Fortunately I had some savings, and I spent whatever I needed just to survive. I bought groceries, paid my rent, and hoped for relief.

There was nothing else to do but surrender, go through the dark tunnel, and hope someone could show me the way out.

3.4

Encountering Inner Space

I had always prided myself on being in control, so when I finally sought professional help it meant that I was completely adrift. Through my ex-girlfriend I found a therapist who shared an important characteristic with me: she was also the child of Holocaust survivors.

Almost immediately this commonality sealed our bond, because as I shared the programming of my parents – their intense fear and revulsion of a world that had been mostly hostile – I knew that she alone could relate to and understand the depth and source of my conditioned beliefs.

This allowed me, as I shall describe, to begin to manage all of the various contradictory "programs" that were loaded into my brain (and body) and begin to find peace.

While neither she nor I had "written the code", I had confidence that she could provide spiritual guidance out of the tunnel – or viewed in another way – "psychological tech support".

When I first came to her office I disgorged all of the problems that I felt were causing my distress. These involved finances and relationships that seemed to have fallen apart.

She told me to remember to breathe, and to try to be quiet – and to give these thoughts some space. Over time I developed a sense of trust, but my symptoms seemed to go on and on.

I was desperate for relief and wailed that the treatment was not helping. She noticed my resistance and asked me to be patient.

But as Eckhart had said, I could not stand myself.

I said, "I'm spending a fortune with you to sort out things I should be able to handle myself. I'm isolated and the only reason you listen to my bullshit is because I pay you."

She looked at me and replied, "That's a new voice. I haven't heard that voice before. You sound angry. Why don't you let me have it?"

And I did. I became even more agitated and asked why we couldn't have a friendship where we were equals instead of a professional relationship? Why did I need to come to her Beverly Hills office and spend as much as I would need for a new car?

Then she asked me to notice that voice. "Do you recognize it?" she asked.

I said, "It was my fear again." I was terrified of what was happening to me. But I could sense that this new, stronger expression of my feelings emanated from either a completely new, or long lost part of me. The fear was no longer in complete control; the voice had taken over as "the master program".

"That voice," she said, "is trying to protect you. You see that, right?" I nodded and she continued.

"It's a very strong voice and I like it," she said, "But do you think it could just go sit on that chair over there, and let us continue? Could you ask it to trust us that far?"

I nodded again. Inside my own mind, I literally asked my fear to take a seat nearby while we continued.

And then I noticed it. "I" was still there, in a peaceful and silent state, feeling some of the tension leave my body. As we continued I became calmer as the fear continued to sit nearby. And then it hit me.

The voice of fear was not me. My father, who had always cautioned me about being vigilant and careful, had drummed the protection it afforded into me. And despite his admonitions and my own best efforts I thought I was facing financial ruin in a chaotic world.

My father had worked very hard after bringing us to America, and had made enough to retire in southern California with my mother. But he was always afraid of what might happen.

One of his favorite aphorisms was always, "Don't take any risks."
And now I saw it clearly. My fear was operating as an extremely powerful, conditioned program.

But it wasn't me. I was still slouched in one chair, but my "fear" was temporarily over in the other chair across the room.

I marveled at this revelation to my therapist, who knew I had been a tech writer. I wondered if "this program" could be "uninstalled".

"You don't want to do that." she said, "Even if you could, which is probably impossible. But you want to watch it, like you moved it to that chair. You want to develop a faculty to notice how you are – moment to moment."

And that became my practice. Slowly I began to notice all of the "I"s that Gurdjieff talked about that arose through triggers or for no apparent reason. And I no longer saw them as "me" but as software programs operating within my brain and body.

My therapist took me deeper – asking first whether I wanted to explore other aspects of my fear program – and I agreed.

I had lost my mother and slowly I worked through the sense of horror I felt about her wartime experiences. It brought up more, very intense feelings of shame, loss, grief and inadequacy.

I told my therapist one of the stories about my mother; how she had been selected to work at Auschwitz while her parents were sent in the other direction – to extermination. She tried to follow them but a Nazi officer slapped her and her glasses dropped to the ground and shattered.

Extremely nearsighted, she struggled into the barracks where she crawled into a bunk with six other girls, all frightened and famished, and there she found a pair of glasses, held together by string, that had allowed her to survive the war and become my mother.

My therapist looked shocked. She recalled that she had taken her own daughter to Auschwitz and while they were walking through the yard, her daughter had moved aside some dirt with her shoe and had found a broken pair of eyeglasses.

Of course I broke down. Someone had really heard my story and it seemed almost otherworldly to have this type of connection.

Were those my mother's lost eyeglasses? The haunting question came up but immediately I stopped looking for the logical explanation and simply felt the moment …

For that brief instant the linear horizontal movement of my life simply stopped and it seemed something from elsewhere – the "vertical dimension" – had entered the room with us.

My therapist smiled and pointed to the window. The sun had broken through a bank of clouds.

Slowly I revealed other layers of the stories that had shaped me, and began to see many of my "agreements," "dreams" and "programs" with greater clarity.

As the long suppressed memories came up they were extremely painful, but instead of letting a commentary about them provide "an explanation" my therapist encouraged me to simply be with them, allowing the emotions to come up. As I had the fear, "I" noticed these emotions and their accompanying sensations and allowed them to play out.

I let all of them course through my body, feeling them and watching them, and marveling at the reality that none of them was ultimately me.

And at the end of each session I realized that through it all, I was still alive. None of these demons had destroyed me. And each time I left my therapist said the same thing, "Be kind to yourself, and remember to breathe."

Instead of now seeing my situation as dire I began to perceive it as a process that was necessary. I still spent a lot of time in bed, and did very little, but I accepted the necessity of what I now termed "self-care".

The little boy crying out inside me needed and deserved my attention and love, and it was time to look inward.

3.5

The Loneliness of Separation

One of the very first things my therapist ever said to me was, "You need other people." I had come to her after breaking up from a very close relationship and suffering from the intense isolation I described above.

These four words reminded me of my solitude and broke me down emotionally, and I began to sob, because I was acutely aware of the many walls I had built up to protect myself and keep myself from feeling hurt.

It was the reason I had wanted to "uninstall Fear" – deep inside I knew what it had cost me.

As I have described, and as my therapist well knew, both of my parents had experienced a horrible world, and each in their own way had tried to educate me with the means for "protection".

For my father accumulation of money meant safety. I discovered this "program" early on in my therapy. Its veracity ("Is it true?") was quickly shattered when my therapist pointed out that my father's financial success (before the war) had not protected him from the Nazis.

My father was meticulous with accounting and scrupulous planning and he had deeply ingrained this discipline in me, for better or worse.

When my girlfriend and I took a trip together at one point she noticed my propensity to try to control every aspect of the trip – where we parked, how far a restaurant was and so on, and she asked me about it.

I described it as my father's mantra, which was "Don't fuck up." (Anticipate every hypothetical eventuality and prepare for it.)

She turned to me and suggested a different mantra: "Let love in."

At the time it sounded "interesting" but my mind quickly rejected it. I reminded myself that I had to remember where the restaurant I had chosen for lunch was located.

Our relationship had reached a point where I had intense resistance; I was listening to the clamor of my mind and finding fault wherever I could.

When I finally broke it off, I thought it would be easy but I discovered that instead, my anxiety became even more acute.

I felt guilty about some things I had said and when I went to see a body worker to try to feel better, she found an energetic blockage in my chest.

I had to come to terms with the reality that my ex-girlfriend and I were still connected and that while I could not manage the sort of conventional relationship that I thought I "should" have, I realized that I did not want to lose the friendship.

Deep down I knew that our intimacy and connection was a program I did not want to uninstall. It wasn't always easy but I missed our talks on the phone and just knowing she was there. Although she often drove me crazy I had to confront the fact that I had lost her, and I missed her.

I had successfully jettisoned the "rescue" and "marriage forever" programs but I could not shake a deep feeling of sadness and loss. It was palpable and something I needed to honor.

But I could not mention my inner conflicts as our friendship continued because I realized that I had hurt her deeply, and if I mentioned what I was feeling she would answer, "But you broke up with me!"

I had to accept the reality that there were feelings inside of me that my conscious mind could not manage or control. My ex was no longer someone to whom I could unburden myself, especially about my isolation and loneliness. I had burned that bridge.

That's why I was paying my therapist.

Later on during my recovery, when I briefly attended sessions at my therapist's home, her small dog was on the back of the couch near my outstretched hand. It began licking my hand and I watched it for a few seconds, and then without thinking, I moved my hand away.

"Why did you do that?" she asked me.

"Do what?" I wondered.

"The dog was showing you affection and you pulled away." she pointed out.

At first I dismissed this idea, but it ultimately led to a deep recognition that in so many ways I had never realized, I did not think I deserved love.

Looking back, this was an example of an If/Then programming statement. If I became rich and famous, I would be deserving of a wonderful family. Alone and ordinary, I considered myself unworthy.

During that same session I recalled how my mother had also tried to prepare me for life and relationships. I don't remember what prompted it but I remembered how she would frequently tell me something like, "If you continue to be a slob no woman will want you."

"Wow," my therapist said. That's all she needed to say.

Another layer of deeply conditioned shame had been exposed. Unless I behaved a certain way and earned a certain amount of money, I was not deserving of love.

Another If/Then statement: If I deviated from certain stringent norms, I would be rejected.

No wonder I was anxious. Most if not all of the cells in my body were sure, based upon these deeply conditioned beliefs that I was going to die destitute and alone.

3.6

Sex as Software

Time to face the truth:

So where exactly **was I** seeking satisfaction or connection?

When we think of our inner functions in terms of software, with DNA as our organic programming language, the extent of our conditioning and automatism is nowhere more evident than in the area of sex.

My first recollection of my sexual program "loading" came when I was about ten years old and my parents took me to a fancy dinner in Manhattan, hosted by my father's best friend … a famous European actor.

I remember being mesmerized and being unable to take my eyes off a statuesque woman in a low cut dress at a nearby table. Tall and big boned she had a regal bearing, and I suddenly noticed new sensations in many parts of my body, but particularly in my underpants. I had discovered "my type".

When I broached the subject with my parents they generally demurred. It wasn't so much that they were prudish or uncomfortable, but rather they believed that sexual awakening was a natural process that would happen in due course.

But as I entered college sex seemed to be happening everywhere except in my dorm room. When I discussed it with my father he seemed unfazed, certain it would happen when it was time. His main concern was that I not contract any diseases or get a girl pregnant, so he told me to always use contraception – which remained the extent of his insight on the subject.

I was jealous of other males I knew who were apparently successful with women, and I went after my "type" with no success and with some absurdly humorous results.

I remember sitting on the toilet in agony my freshman year of college when my dorm advisor found me and explained that I was suffering from "blue balls". I knew what to do all too well at that point.

I was always looking for perfection, and never finding (or accepting) -- to the point where my college friends kidded me about the number of "mixers" I attended.

When I travelled to Europe during two summers my father encouraged me to "sow my oats" as he had as a young man on the Riviera, with his best friend the actor, and told me of his own adventures.

I had enormous respect for my father and wanted to please him, so losing my virginity took on enormous importance, as it also did with respect to my peer group at college. But in conversations with my father about women he told me "You have to dominate a woman."

I didn't really understand this because he did not dominate my mother; it seemed to me that they had a marriage where they listened and respected one another deeply. Moreover I had many talks with my mother and I knew her to be very strong, and also that she often got her way.

In addition I was becoming increasingly aware of the submissive tendencies in my own sexual fantasies so I was quite confused. So when I spent two summers in Europe and returned with my virginity intact it took a heavy mental toll.

At one point, I invested 50 dollars in a hooker in the Red Light Zone in Amsterdam but her vulgarity and impatience was a huge turnoff, and when she tugged at my penis like she was trying to start an outboard motor I fled back to my hostel mortified by the experience.

At long last I finally lost my virginity on my 23rd birthday when I was working as a tour guide in Acapulco … in a job where it seemed almost a requirement to have a series of affairs. But I was also very lonely.

And as I grew older my type crystallized. I continued to sense a clear and powerful chemical attraction (DNA?) to tall and powerful women. I fantasized about wrestlers and eventually discovered Bondage, Domination and Sado-Masochism (BDSM), and was repulsed and ashamed of my yearnings to be sensually controlled.

I could not begin to comprehend my powerful attraction to images of women who dressed in leather, would treat me like a dog, put me on a leash, possibly beat me, and turn me into a slave.

(In those days pictures like these were hard to come by – now they are the norm.)

But where were these bizarre thoughts and feelings coming from?

I had "vanilla" relationships with women who fit my type superficially but if I mentioned my fantasies they generally laughed or recoiled, so I kept my desires as "movies in my head," fueling my occasional affairs and sexual encounters.

As the women's movement gained steam, any mention of fantasies was seriously attacked as "objectification", and I was afraid of humiliation by someone I inadvertently offended.

As I listened to women in the course of friendship, relationship and in society at large, I recognized that it was precisely this sort of objectification which triggered their "pain bodies" (Eckhart Tolle's term) and ran counter to their apparent female programming in a way that I found hard to comprehend.

Feminism and the Sexual Revolution aside, through my job as a tour guide and later as I grew older and more experienced, I also became acutely aware that casual sex was not as "okay" with most women as I had been led to believe by the mass media and the "Playboy philosophy".

Even when they said otherwise, a deep bond (chemical and psychological) generally developed for the women I encountered with any sexual relationship – a bond that needed to be honored.

Sometimes I thought it must be the women I chose, or who chose me, but the more experience I garnered the more the truth became apparent: most men and women are running different sexual programs. ("Men are from Mars, Women are from Venus")

Even women who came to the resorts in which I worked in my twenties for a "last fling" found it difficult and painful to leave their lovers behind. Part of that was doubtless the fantasy and allure of the lush environment but I knew it ran much deeper. As much as they wanted to be able to screw and move on, women I knew and spoke with about the subject had a different set of values.

While the clichéd view of gender preference is that males want sex and women want security or money it seemed to me that what women really wanted was the security of connection. And deep inside it seemed to me that they wanted it all – the lifelong commitment – and for that I needed the *perfect* woman.

But honoring the feminine perspective was not very good for my sex life. It seemed as though the more respectful I was the more I got rejected or relegated to the dreaded friend zone.

And then of course I discovered porn – first in magazines and books and later in video and online. Far easier than dating or "relationships" I found that I could still get very aroused by looking at certain kinds of pictures. The sexual software loaded with regularity and there were also marijuana, which made it even more intense.

With the rise of the Internet I found I could get almost anything I wanted and, still ashamed, would revert to my porn collection on my computer when I got lonely or bored.

I also had one occasion I will never forget, when a series of images suddenly came up for a few seconds while teaching PowerPoint® – fortunately the person I was with was a good friend and after promising I would be more discreet in the future, she was willing to overlook it and we shared a laugh.

"Professor PowerPoint®" was busted.

After my parents died and I had a bit of money I carefully experimented with professionals in the BDSM field, attempting to form a friendship or relationship with a woman who manifested "my type" but with whom I could also find warmth, affection and communication.

In other words, not just looking for the proverbial hooker "with a heart of gold" that you so often find in fiction; but in my case I was seeking a loving dominatrix.

I also found compassion for others with sexual programming that made them pariahs in society; I began to comprehend the plight of gays and I was very relieved that my own sexual conditioning did not lead to an attraction for underage girls or boys.

And I discovered over and over again that the reality of gratuitous sex was not as satisfying as the powerfully programmed fantasy – and even when it was sexually intense, the satisfaction was fleeting, and afterwards there was almost always a feeling of revulsion and emptiness.

It became increasingly clear that the mental fantasy was powerful, but the actual realization with a person who was essentially a stranger, was awkward and pointless.

But this recognition came only when I had allowed myself to experience what I had lusted for without guilt or shame.

My fantasies became clearer as I studied them objectively. I found German women particularly attractive which also troubled me because of my parents' experiences during WWII, and I was ashamed that I was apparently attracted to women who represented their worst fears.

I also found myself attracted to black women. One reason seemed their unattainability; which was the case, looking back, when I lusted after a librarian in Junior High School. When I worked in the Caribbean these feelings surfaced frequently, but I was much too ashamed and terrified to follow through.

Finally in semi-retirement in Las Vegas, after doing much of the work described here, I decided to lose any sense of shame and allow these feelings to find expression, hopefully without getting murdered or robbed.

I met a young black escort online and we became friendly when I visited her at a strip club and would bring her lunch.

Her story reminded me of films I had seen and stories I had heard about the dark side of the sex trade. She had been sold to a pimp at 14 and while she now seemed independent she had no other way to earn a decent living. Well-spoken and intelligent, she had so much potential and we became better friends based upon our respective needs.

At this time I shut off all of the warning voices in my head and simply went with the experience. All along my mind warned me that I was being used, taking insane risks and being a fool.

Of course I had to help her financially but she always said that she didn't want to ask me for money – which might have been part of her "act" – but I found in her a willing partner to explore what I was looking for.

What I discovered was that I really craved the feeling of the physical closeness between us and the fact that we got along made me feel good. She would come over and do her laundry and we would talk. I treated her respectfully and I tried to make her life easier. Of course we had fun.

We still correspond but I can't help noticing that the sexual urge subsided since I had grown closer to her – as it had with other women who had fulfilled the fantasy and become friends. With friendship the fire abated.

But I discovered several things. First of all this was almost entirely mechanical. Whether with porn or in person "I" had very little to do with the sexual experiences that occurred.

This also served to reduce the fear of sexual inadequacy and impotence that had plagued me since college. Finally recognizing that no one was in control relieved me of a burden I had carried since those days when I hoped to please my father and impress my peers.

I also found that there was an immense satisfaction in not listening to the fear voice that tried to dissuade me, and then coming away from an experience without getting murdered or robbed.

Layla represented every fantasy that I had yearned to fulfill through porn – and I could feel the desire begin to fade as the reality of driving her home and deal with her "drama" replaced the fleeting release of stress and the pleasure I experienced when in her company.

And at one point when I lay next to this luscious, large and curvy young black woman I thought, "Mommy" – so there it was.

The Jewish stereotype was solidified – and it was part of my software – my DNA.

I chuckled quietly to myself as I caressed the nape of her neck.

Others may now refer to my programming as "sexual addiction" and to the extent that it might have ruined my life, they may have a point. But single and unfettered in my middle age there was no career to threaten or marriage to destroy.

Eventually my young friend moved away and I had neither been busted nor arrested. I counted my blessings, kept in touch, and decided that once was probably enough.

Ironically, today, it is clear that I share my "bizarre" preferences with a majority of heterosexual males -- who have very specific turn-ons that they did not choose, but which heighten their sexual pleasure. The imagery of fetishes, bondage and domination has made its way from fringe rock bands to the world of fashion and now into the mainstream.

Unfortunately, what I believe many feminists refer to, as objectification is a big part of what many men seem to find most exciting.

And what most women see as "no games" – commitment or a real relationship – is of interest to men only with a woman who truly "gets" their inner yearnings and doesn't shame them.

Women don't want to be objectified but men want to comfortably be themselves and not play a role in order to get their needs met.

So I decided that since my proclivities are not harmful to anyone else, and I am not married (fortunately) to someone that they may offend, why not pursue them? Why should I settle for unfulfilling sexual experiences?

Because I am thorough in my research, I became very well versed in the BDSM and porn scene and it amazed me that there were apparently thousands of men who were willing to pay for "financial domination" and even undergo chastity.

Within the world of porn there is every possible fantasy, but I was shocked to discover that the movies I played in my head were actually quite tame. While I seemed to prefer "tease and denial" mixed with warmth and affection, on the fringes of the "scene" there were some truly bizarre activities, which other men paid for handsomely.

My "research" took me to domination "trade shows" where there were seminars on things like knife play and elaborate rope bondage.

When I was also exposed to the world of financial domination, where women receive money for absolutely nothing and sometimes are even paid to commit blackmail or take over their "slave's" computers and bank accounts.

Fortunately my interests have not led me to financial ruin. I may be foolish but not stupid. And another lesson my father taught me was not to throw my money away.

But I was truly fascinated by this aspect of who I appeared to be that I had long suppressed – what some psychologists refer to as the *shadow*.

"The *shadow*, said celebrated Swiss psychiatrist C.G. Jung, is the unknown "dark side" of our personality – dark both because it tends to consist predominantly of the primitive, negative, socially or religiously depreciated human emotions and impulses like sexual lust, power strivings, selfishness, greed, envy, anger or rage, and due to its unenlightened nature, completely obscured from consciousness."

– Psychology Today

3.7

The Power of Sexual Imagery

I continued to be fascinated by my discoveries. My fantasies were never what I would have chosen; instead they emanated from a very dark and mysterious place.

Sadomasochistic images, which were once just in comic books and the occasional fashion ad, now flood advertising and movies and are prevalent in rock music. Everywhere you look there is an emphasis on degradation, control and power.

This speaks to what Eckhart Tolle calls the "collective pain body" or emotional programming and is the deep conditioning passed on genetically, connecting the accumulated trauma of past generations (like my parents' experiences of Nazi occupied Europe). Eckhart also refers to the collective pain bodies over centuries of abuse of women, Native Americans and blacks.

At one time I was deeply ashamed of my desires and my propensity for strange behavior like being put on a leash and walked like a dog, but now through the Internet I became aware of just how prevalent (and common) this programming is.

So I became aware of what makes me tick but also cognizant of how negatively it is viewed by most of the women I'm likely to meet. There's also much vulnerability because without a loving and understanding partner, I may become susceptible to manipulation by "professionals" who would use my desires to support themselves at my considerable expense.

But the energy of the fantasy is palpable and as my libido subsides in older age, I want this excitement in my lovemaking. And I have no more guilt and shame about it because it is clearly not "me" – it is thoroughly programmed.

Looking back so much is now clear. I had had intense feelings of submission (which I could barely understand) in my old day job as a legal secretary – thoroughly enjoying my work whenever I could earn the appreciation of a hot female attorney with my attentiveness and competence.

My submissive tendency has also served me well in some relationships. My desire to please my partner is deep and genuine and so there have been women with whom I have bonded intensely – but whom I have also deeply disappointed when the flame went out.

At this point I would love to find a partner and experience this level and intensity of sexuality within the context of a "real relationship" – along with the other aspects that I've discovered I need for emotional nourishment: loving affection and warmth.

I've also come to recognize that most relationships are energetic mine fields unless we remain present. When the flame flickers and dies the pain body gets triggered.

We all come with baggage and sooner or later expectations, which went unsaid, are unfulfilled. That is when the voice in the head gets more vocal and pain bodies get triggered.

Here is what my inner voice generally cautions me about:

I begin to feel that on some level we're not in sync. It could well be a function of my European background, with a distinct intellectual snobbery, but when I don't feel that my intellect and dark sense of humor are appreciated, I tend to bolt. Or as my therapist said, "cut and run".

Of course this is an obvious consequence of listening to my voice of fear or inner programming. Often I can hear one of my parents speaking and suggesting that the person I'm with is not worthy – or that it's me who is undeserving or as my therapist aptly put it, "less than".

And now I've come to realize, this is a recipe for loneliness.

Through my inner work I've identified the two "programs" that lead to the most suffering:
1. The search for "true love"; and
2. The quest for material success and its seeming security.

I've finally reached the point where I understand that it's this very intense "need" and the "search" that causes suffering – it is not the circumstances of life but rather the conditioned belief system that creates misery.
I sometimes still think that perhaps when seen objectively these programs can eventually be "deleted" or reprogrammed – but the palpable power of the sexual program is an important lesson.

In my lived experience – as opposed to my fantasy life, I've finally found that the most powerful "executable" leading to deep fulfillment, is a deep connection with warmth, empathy and affection.

If sexual connection becomes part of the experience it may be even better, but a night of laughter with good friends who enjoy my company is the most nourishing way I have found to spend my time.

But the demons can be teachers and deserve further scrutiny. As I found in therapy, honesty and objective self-observation brings some interesting discoveries, so let's dig a bit deeper.

3.8

Sub Space

There is still more to tell about my foray into submissive fantasies. As noted above, I've found tremendous relief about being open about my sexual preferences, and fortunately they are not currently illegal.

BDSM has been around for a long time, and currently this "scene" may be one of the most perfect examples of the economic law of supply and demand.

There are a relatively few hot, savvy women who truly understand the many males who are programmed to lust after and worship them. The sheer number of porn sites and ads online, many by escorts who have seen the golden goose by simply looking hot and demanding cash for "obedience," is amazing.

If the reader is still unaware of this phenomenon, there are scores of women who practice "financial domination" and receive money over the Internet for doing nothing more than posting pictures – sometimes actually of themselves.

And there is apparently no shortage of men willing to contribute to the lifestyles of these hot women, as you can readily see if you follow one of the dominant females on Twitter.

Almost always the attraction seems to be the ability to give up control. Many ads appeal to executives and professional men who are powerful in their jobs, and maintain a strong image within conventional relationships (many are married and this indiscretion is fraught with danger).

Finally, helping sex addicts recover has become a growth industry.

But for those with this kind of conditioning, there's a tremendous release of energy in the company of a beautiful woman who seems to know you intuitively, and who makes all of the decisions.

Many of these women eschew "sexual services" to avoid legal problems, but they still present a tremendous turn on for the many men who are willing to spend serious cash to be in their company, even briefly.

That's the problem. It's addictive and expensive.

When I finally decided to experiment in this world to see where it led, I discovered that for brief periods, being in "sub space" (out of control) has a lightness that is unparalleled in the modern world.

Not being obliged to "keep my shit together" is truly a relief. Especially when so much of my programming has been about not screwing up.

You can lose yourself in sub space briefly, but it's costly and ultimately empty. When the experience ends all you are left with is a memory, which can feel sublime until you receive your monthly bank statement.

But it's no wonder that many wealthy men take advantage of the availability of professionals, in BDSM and in "normal sexual encounters" to simply avoid the drama of relationships, and being sucked into situations which trigger one's own – or a partner's – pain body.

When I moved to Vegas I was fortunate enough to be able to afford a few flings, but I discovered quickly that very few such professionals could make you really suspend your disbelief.

The reality is far different from the fantasy; when you catch yourself with a collar attached to a leash, kissing some stranger's feet, and you realize deep down that you really don't want to be there ... You feel really fucking stupid.

Unless you can completely let go and enter sub space, the fantasy evaporates. Then, during that brief period, the Ego is silent as your own needs are completely suppressed to please the "Goddess".

But the amazing thing is that for many men even humiliation is a turn on. It's a deep paradox and can be a source of shame, but it's undeniable once experienced.

In perusing ads and web sites online I discovered many areas of amazing excitement that made me squeamish …

Do I really want to be slapped? The video turns me on – the reality not so much.

I can run the movie in my head or look at pictures that are shocking and get very aroused and also relaxed in ways that are difficult to attain with "a real woman".

And this makes "real women" – especially those my age that feel invisible as a result, furious, and I and understand that.

But it does not change the plumbing, or the underlying reality that when one finds something that is a powerful turn on, one pursues it. The intellect is temporarily suspended, which can feel exhilarating.

In my case this has led to some painfully humorous encounters, in strip clubs and in private, where I've tried to get romantically involved with women who have zero interest in anything except getting paid, not laid.

What can happen, even when you become friends (and I have) is that now the reality of the "world" intercedes. You quickly discover that these fantasy women have real lives that are often very real and troubled, and that you are easily drawn into their drama.

Another conditioned program that can take over at that point is to become the knight in shining armor – or the rescuer – but that can get even more problematic and expensive.

So I would find myself doing the same thing I was doing in "real relationships" when the shit hit the fan – I would cut and run. Of course now, when the exchange was "professional" it was much easier, and there was little or no guilt. Exactly because there were "no strings", I was free to bolt.

One woman once told me that was what the "donation" was for – since she was receiving "fair value" for her services the client was free to go his own way any time.

But what I noticed was that despite this apparent liberty I wanted to be "more than" a client.

For me each of these women were and are still people, so surprisingly feelings of regret would linger.

It is also interesting that for me it is only within BDSM that I've found a comfortable place to be pleasing to a woman, and even chivalrous in the romantic tradition. Doing so with many "modern" women seems to make them feel I'm too sensitive and not sufficiently alpha.

Or they believe that something must be expected in return – and of course that makes them into "the other kind" of woman.

One of the places I have met women who are open to alternative relationships is at parties geared to foot fetish devotees. I found it sublimely amusing that when I went to those web sites to see which women might attend I was greeted with pictures of … feet.

At fetish parties I discovered an interesting mix of women (many of them materially motivated to be sure) with whom I could play out my desires without judgment. I could have wonderful conversations and even bond sensually while I rubbed lotion on their feet or massaged their shoulders and necks.

And again, within this scene I often tried to find a romantic partner – with mostly comedic results. The language of BDSM and the fetish world may be obedience and chivalry but the currency is always cash.

But confronting my conditioning and shame, and allowing the energy to flow freely was quite liberating.

And of course I would continually wonder just what it was that made me want to feel "less than"; to be controlled sensually, and to relinquish my "manhood".

As I watched myself in these situations I would ask: "Why did I continue to seek and worship the unattainable?"

Energetically this turned out to be the same thing that I eventually found with the spiritual search; oddly there is the discovery that **it is search itself that you are addicted to**.

With the easy availability of the Internet many men find a lover or a "real relationship" only to still peruse the singles sites or fantasize about new encounters when they want distraction.

I remember how Hugh Grant was engaged to one of the most beautiful women in the world and was arrested for soliciting a transsexual in Hollywood.

Real relationships are hard to sustain.

It's hard enough to become comfortable with your own programming, but accepting the conditioned insanity of a partner is hard. I am in awe of my happily married friends.

Fueling the libido is wonderful but you can't be sexually charged all the time – especially as you get older. But with age comes a great deal of self-doubt. For a middle-aged man getting a nice erection is reassuring, which is why we sometimes do so many really stupid things.

Once the libido has expressed itself, it's really nice if, once in a while, your partner brings you a sandwich. And then, as anyone who understands most male sexual programming knows – "Please be quiet and leave me alone to bask in my maleness."

Or if I am still in sub space or just feeling the love, I will gladly get up and take care of my partner's needs. During the sexual or infatuation phase everyone is charming.

But by now it should be clear that I've never been married. The conditioned pattern I've been following is the search for the "right" woman – or so I thought. But ultimately I don't like the deal as it seems to be structured in America today. And the exit clause, especially if there are children, can be both painful and lead to a lifetime of indentured servitude.

The fantasy of slavery is fun for a while – the reality not so much.

But I can certainly see why so many women are angry. Male sexual programming is contradictory, often self-defeating and calculated to ultimately leave us isolated and alone.

But sometimes we like it that way.

3.9

The Solace of Solitude

My mother, who knew me rather well, would ask me sometimes what I was doing that night and when I said "nothing" she would say sagely – "Yes, you need your peace".

But I was conditioned to believe I could not be happy without a companion. I idealized my parents and their relationship, and no actual connection that I ever found matched the fantasy about their union that I carried in my head.

When I broke up with my girlfriend in 2008, I discovered the bliss of solitude – not so much because of her but – as I later realized – I could suspend my attachment to my frantic thinking mind.

I no longer needed to think about the relationship. Part of the constant mental chatter was about getting what I thought to be sexual gratification. Much more was about not stepping in land mines that would lead to angry or uncomfortable confrontations.

I had originally approached my ex online because of her appearance, but over nine months, as we had grown close intellectually and emotionally, our respective pain bodies became activated more and more often.

I had also shared my sexual fantasies with her; she physically represented the type of tall powerful women to whom I was strongly attracted.

But as she shared some of her negative experiences with other online contacts and complained that many of the men wanted her to wrestle them down, and do "other weird things", it became clear that the very things that turned me on made her uncomfortable.

Nevertheless I tried to broach the topic of my own sexual desires and she seemed open, but her response was to find humor in the "scene" and laughingly suggest that I needed a spanking or otherwise feign an attempt at BDSM, as she understood it.

This playfulness was always done with warmth and laughter, but while I knew she was not ridiculing me, it was a huge turnoff and disappointment. It made me question her open-mindedness and even her feelings for me.

For my part I wanted very much to understand her sexuality, but unfortunately she had had some very traumatic experiences as a young girl, and that door was not one either of us wanted to open.

So I tried to make it work, as did she but when the pressures of our respective lives got more challenging, I did what I was used to – I broke it off.

Looking back it was certainly a case allowing our two "pain bodies" to go out of control; neither of us were "present" in the relationship as compared to our inner voices clamoring for attention and satisfaction.

She once said to me, after we broke up, that I never really dated her – I dated the idea of her that only existed in my head. As I continued my work in self-observation and growth her assessment became more and more insightful.

When I began working in an Eckhart Tolle group I became even more deeply conscious of the role my inner voice played in keeping me oblivious to reality – and alone.

But of course I continued to seek distraction so as not to confront the void that I felt in my isolation. The monkey-mind continually looks for other kinds of "entertainment".

3.10

Gambling and Numbers

(Chance v. Intention)

I idolized my father and wanted desperately to make him proud of me. Among my inner "programs" the strongest compulsion seemed to be trying to make up for parents' misfortunes and horrific experiences.

My therapist once summarized: "So your father insisted that you work hard and be disciplined to become important and successful, but also you were supposed to enjoy life and be a playboy."

Yup.

A wonderful memory of my father was when I was in high school and played a bit of pool, and my father told me that pool was "nothing" and he took me to a pool hall where we found the only billiard table.

He had played in coffee houses in Vienna and when he chalked up his cue stick I figured this would be a boring afternoon because I knew nothing about three cushion billiards.

But suddenly this man who was then as old as I am now (67) proceeded to impart ungodly spin to the one white ball, get it to strike the other, bounce with geometric perfection against three surfaces, and then strike the other ball. Over and over again he succeeded with a wry smile as I watched agape, each time leaving his cue ball in perfect position.

The other game I watched him play when I worked in casino hotels and he came to visit was Roulette. He had played in Monte Carlo with his famous friend and now I watched his careful demeanor and his "rules".

When my father lost his limit, which was ten dollars, he left. No cajoling would make him continue. But when he won, he left with cash in his pocket, and a wry smile.
I had gambled a bit in Vegas on my brief visits, but when I moved there I knew that if I got "the fever" I would lose. They did not build the hotels and casinos from winners …

I tried to remain present and watch my "self" as I played and since I was now a resident, whenever I won a bit, I cashed out and left.

Somehow the chaos or chance of numbers intrigued me, and I noticed that the angst of losing far exceeded the satisfaction of winning.

Then I realized that as football season began I could watch the game with "skin in the game" and I enjoyed it more.

I did not strongly "identify" with any city or franchise. I found it laughable that people would watch in blistering cold, with painted faces and understood that "fan" was short for fanatic.

But I enjoyed wagering on teams based upon my expectations and I noticed that when I won the voice in my head would congratulate "me" on "my" cleverness.

Or when I lost, the same voice got a lot of satisfaction and energy from berating "me" as a loser or a victim,

As I watched a game on TV, I noticed myself getting angry at "bad calls" and "stupid decisions" – making one judgment after another about what was essentially a meaningless event.

And yet, with some objectivity, I was also able to observe and recognize that neither my reactions nor my preconceived notions had any impact on the outcome of a game.

This was not an If/Then causal situation. Whatever "I" wanted was irrelevant to the outcome.

And yet the outcome seemed so significant to others. The players and their fans were rabid in their desire for victory. TV commentary before and after a game went on for hours.

Inside my "self" there was more measured reaction. I never bet much but my Ego was on the line and I became aware of several truths:

The first was the palpable satisfaction of my Ego and its smugness if I won.

And second, I began to see how arbitrary the notion of winning really was. Back in college a fraternity brother I looked up to segmented everyone he knew into winners and losers. Throughout my life that distinction has remained with me, and my experiences with women generally made me feel like a loser.

I've spent a great deal of my life struggling to achieve the status of a winner and it's exhausting.

Gambling provided the clarity to realize, that the energy of losing, is paradoxically, equally powerful.

As I had discovered, the gut level feeling of any loss, and the resulting feeling of being a victim has a strange allure.

And professional sports have some odd aspects. For one thing when an athlete thanks "God" for winning, I wondered whose God the other team had prayed to.

And now as I examined my own actions I saw that the entire notion of winning and losing was an abstract, conceptual fantasy.

3.11

That Moment When You Know You "Won"

Here is how it worked one particular day. I discovered how "winning" was completely different for "me" than it was for the thousands of fans who were watching the same football game in New Jersey.

I had taken "+4 ½ points" on the New York Giants who were behind by 21 points. The Giants came back and with the game tied at 24 the Carolina Panthers lined up for a field goal.

At that moment I realized I had "won" – whether they made the field goal (a big deal for them because they would remain undefeated) or whether they missed and the Giants won (keeping them in playoff contention) -- it made no difference whatsoever to me.

Three points either way meant everything to millions of people around the country, especially in Charlotte and at the Meadowlands where the game was played. But I sat back and watched the kick with detachment. I had won my ten bucks.

What a dramatic contrast to my usual reactive conditioning. No longer subject to a good or bad outcome, I saw clearly the relative nature of all judgment and the absolute role of perspective.

Another aspect of my perspective was this – how much did I risk on this game?

Suppose, now living in Vegas, I was a really addicted gambler, and I had wagered a year's income, or in my case, even more dramatically, lost my social security check.

Certainly my identification with the outcome would be much more intense. But in my case I had bet ten bucks to win $9.55 – not exactly my life savings – but enough to make me notice my attachment and its intensity. As the Giants came back and I began to recognize that what I thought was a "lost" bet was turning around and I might "win" my inner state turned positive.

And the series of plays that resulted in my win were even more exciting because in some ways my "smarts" were on the line.

Instead of being a dope I was now a "winner".

And the recognition of the precise moment when my mind first registered the certainty of the positive outcome (even though the "real" game was still in doubt) was palpable.

What I also noticed was the friction of "not knowing" – that interval when the "outcome" is in doubt and there's a churning in your stomach. This is a visceral sensation that seems to convince you that it is "You" – it puts "you" in the "game".

But upon further reflection it can't be "you" because then, once again, who would be there to notice the change?

Of course all of these programs are deeply conditioned in our culture, and I marvel at their complexity and power.

It makes me wonder about sports in other civilizations. We know the Mayans had an enormous ball court and there are various theories about what games might have been played there. It's interesting to speculate, especially with the Mayans' sophisticated mathematical knowledge, how a completely different spiritual and scientific psychology might have operated within such a game.

Understanding their psychology might show either the commonality or the diversity of potential for the human organism in terms of what is perceived as "victory".

One thing becomes clear. The mind (and body) love to experience the intensity of winning, and even losing, and their level of force is connected to one essential component – risk.

3.12

Higher Risk

One might ask how I can credibly describe levels of risk with the laughable amount I wagered on the football game.

(I'm keenly aware that even ten dollars is not laughable to a large percentage of people who live paycheck to paycheck.)

I am indeed very fortunate to have not experienced the situation or circumstance where ten dollars was the difference between eating and not eating.

One of the major aspects of the work I have done and where I am today is to develop a profound sense of gratitude for the blessings I've received.

But when my income dried up and all I was receiving was social security, I began to seriously consider risk in terms of "investing".

At first my risk tolerance was very low. I had already lost money on Wall Street after my father had admonished me never to go into stocks. The intense guilt from that result – because much of the money I had lost was actually earned by my father – it contributed to my subsequent anxiety and depression.

So having recognized that deep layer of conditioning, I decided to experiment with risk again … but this time hopefully, more consciously.

The reality was that rather than being "conscious", I instead succumbed to another rather common but very powerful program – greed.

I had enough to live comfortably but I wanted more. Now living in Las Vegas there were many new temptations that I thought would provide pleasure, but they cost more money than I wanted (or thought I could afford) to spend.

After doing more research and consulting with financial advisors I went back into the stock market, and lost another chunk.

This time I was "present" for the reaction – and could feel the intense lump in my gut and the resulting inability to sleep while my Ego lambasted me for my stupidity.

Seeing the loss in perspective I managed to recover a bit. I also "confessed" my findings to a spiritual teacher specializing in addiction (Scott Kiloby) and learned that my experience was not uncommon among seekers of "enlightenment".

There is a term called "spiritual bypass" which is when you think that now you've "transcended" feeling or doing anything stupid because you've "awakened".

The reality is quite the opposite. When you do something patently stupid, like lose a chunk of cash in a casino or the stock market, it's gambling, and a deep pit forms in your stomach and you hate yourself intensely.

I now knew from personal experience that this feeling was palpable and real. I had to own it and continue to feel it until it subsided. And then I had to find the will to do it responsibly, or not at all.

Did I or did I not have the "free will" to resist the temptation to try for a big score?

I still felt like a fool, but I determined to limit my risk to sums that would not hurt. As I had seen in therapy, pain can be a wonderful teacher.

With gambling of any kind, there is obviously no guarantee as to the outcome. One thing I've noticed is that I have certain tendencies – like the sexual proclivities I already described – that seem to run "on their own".

When gambling it became very obvious that life without a safety net – and truly experiencing "not knowing" – was again both exciting and addictive.

It's no wonder that literature is full of characters who "risk it all". But from my father I had learned to temper my risk-taking so as not to jeopardize my comfort and security.

The mythology of males who'll crash their ships on rocks to approach the siren's song or Circe's spell, exists for a reason: some forms of self-destruction have an unmistakable attraction.

So I watched myself win and lose and felt the results. Winning never felt as good – as losing felt bad.

But there was also an unmistakable rush from losing – and feeling the victim – which I recognized but did not quite understand.

It seemed that as my mind reeled with self-blame and a search of explanation there was a release of energy that kept bringing me back for more. My mind was addicted to the attention.

The other alluring aspect of gambling relates to what some call the "Clever Boy" program.

This is the program that suggests that if we "win" it serves to confirm a belief that we're smarter than others.

Since we want to believe ourselves to be mentally superior, we begin to try to repeat experiences that confirm our brilliance – and making money without effort makes us think we're particularly clever.

I am not sure whether many women are programmed in this way but obviously the casinos and all of the sweepstakes offers, rely on it heavily. All it takes is a few major losses to begin to convince us that our brilliance is overrated – something my father told me frequently.

The other major insight to be gained from watching oneself gamble, whether in a casino or the stock market is that it challenges our most basic psychological tendencies:

Greed, the Ego's clamor for more, impatience and desire for control all rise to the surface when money (material security) is on the line; but the one thing that must go is attachment to the "me" or what "I want NOW" – because that leads to the delusion of imminent expectation.

If we can put the "me" aside we can survive in a casino and perhaps even on Wall Street.

I decided that the lessons learned were invaluable but I did not need to keep returning to the ledge. But what prepared me for accepting real emotional risk was perhaps the biggest leap of faith I ever took – trusting my intuition!

3.13

The Year of the Cat

Recalling my experience with her dog – where I had removed my hand from receiving affection, my therapist suggested that I should find a way to shift my attention away from myself and adopt a dog.

I had always wanted a dog and considered getting a pooch because I trusted my therapist implicitly. But I wondered whether I was ready to be woken up each morning by a hungry and noisy little creature I would have to walk and clean up after.

Which, of course, was precisely her point.

Eventually I settled on possibly getting a cat; I had been a temporary caretaker for cats and liked them because they seemed low maintenance. I spent several months visiting shelters and almost adopting several animals. But each time I seemed to find a convenient excuse to back out.

Finally I went to the West LA shelter to look at a cute dog I had seen online – but was turned off by the massive barking in the kennel. As I left, for some reason I decided to check out the cat room.

There was a sweet middle-aged volunteer working that Thursday and she asked me what I was looking for.

"A Maine Coon", I said, adding, "I would love an affectionate cat."

Without missing a beat she opened a cage and said, "This is a very sweet cat." She reached in and put a scruffy emaciated and frightened little tabby into my arms.

The cat pushed its nose under my armpit and butted me with her head.

"She likes you", the lady said.

I shook my head but realized that this was heading in a dangerous direction. We took her into the exercise room where she ran around and finally jumped into my lap and let me stroke her soft fur. I realized that if I was serious about this step, this was it.

I decided then that I would take her home, and the lady told me to take care of the paperwork while she got the cat ready for transport. When I was filling out the forms, she appeared in the doorway with a box with air holes.

Suddenly a guy in a white coat appeared and introduced himself as the vet. He said the cat had a small infection and would need some drops.

Moment of truth … last chance to back out and the perfect excuse … just bolt for the door and never look back!

But inside a voice said, "Do it!" I will never forget it. The voice was a new voice again – not my ordinary inner drone.

I took the boxed cat across the street, and dealt with my growing anxiety as I sat by while she was examined. I was already beginning to have regrets when the exam ended, and I bought some drops to administer to her.

When I got her home she was very scared but ate some food, drank some water and then it was time to give her the drops. I picked her up and tried to open her mouth, but she managed to spray most of the drops around the room.

She was also supposed to have a cone around her head to keep from scratching the infected area, but I could not bear to see her in discomfort and took it off of her.

Over the next few months she did some things that if I had known she was prone to do, I would not have taken her – but by that time I was smitten. When she tore up a roll of toilet paper or puked on the rug, I just laughed and cleaned it up.

With the love I was feeling for this little creature I was learning to accept many things that I knew I could not control.

And I couldn't make her love me.
She never again jumped into my lap – the only time had been that moment in the shelter – but she came around in her own time, would head-butt me, lie down beside me and lick me and I would melt.

Now I melt every morning when I get up to scratch her back and give her treats. I have managed to enjoy all of the unexpected things my cat does.

She has taught me love and acceptance in a way I had never dreamed possible, and as my ex-girlfriend suggested I had changed my mantra – I was letting love in.

It wasn't an easy process and there was much resistance but that day in the West LA animal shelter changed my life.

I said no to the fearful voice in my head, and silently went with a deeper knowing.

That's why adopting a cat changed my life. It altered my daily experience in ways that are unfathomable without engaging the other part of the brain – that part that laughs at the cat's antics, loves the feel of its fur, and is constantly surprised by its independent being and vitality, and particularly relishes its love as it licks my hand or nose in greeting and warmth.

The bond with my cat is purely emotional. In fact when I consider how it has affected some of my freedom, my mind will still sometimes raise objections.

But the cat had changed my qualia – my day-to-day experience was improving, but of course a big part of me still wanted answers to questions that had haunted me for a long time.

3.14

Accepting not Knowing

Eventually my anxiety eased enough to allow me to cut back on my expensive therapy. My therapist also travelled abroad and had us meet via Skype. At one point she was in the Arab territories of Israel and I was on my couch in Los Angeles. In the background I heard popping sounds and I asked her what they were. She told me with equanimity that they were artillery fire and gunshots. Nothing unusual in her world …

But still, I was a terrified soul ensnared by my own fearful voice on my couch in West LA – amazing.

During this time I recognized that I needed more people I could talk to. I went on the Internet and discovered a bi-monthly Santa Monica group devoted to the work of Eckhart Tolle.

At the third or fourth meeting the leader of the group, Michael Jeffreys, got into an exchange with an engineer who was asking a series of theoretical psychological questions about "awakening".

Michael asked the engineer whether he could just accept not knowing. As he asked the question he turned to me, and I realized I was shaking my head vehemently.

"So Tom," Michael said, "I guess not knowing is hard for you?"

I nodded vigorously and then I broke out in laughter, as did the entire group. Tension streamed from my body as I recognized two very significant programs:
> I craved the security of certainty; and
> I had not laughed with that kind of intensity in many months.

But Michael pointed out one of the key aspects of Eckhart Tolle's work: that while the voice in the head demands answers and has theories, none of us really know what will happen.

It reminded me of when I asked my therapist a series of questions and then she would reply – even as a renowned neuroscientist, "we really don't know very much."

All we really know, as I had discovered in my therapist's office, is that we are here right now, and we're aware of being here. Everything else is really noise.

The silence that followed the revelation of my (and the group's) discomfort with the unknown reminded me of the peace I had found with my therapist when she would have me stop and create some "space" for whatever had come up.

I later agreed to a series of private sessions with Michael and we met at a lovely park. Again I poured out my problems and stories and then we sat in silence for a few minutes. It was very quiet in the park except for some people chatting in the distance, and some ducks quacking in a pond.

As my mind continued to race about all of the issues I was concerned with, Michael asked me to just stop for a moment – as my therapist had – and to just notice …

"What is the difference," he asked "between the sounds you are listening to in the head, and the voices of those people and quacking of the ducks?"

And it struck me. From an objective perspective there was no difference. I was "aware" of all of the noises in exactly the same way. They were all being interpreted as sound by my brain, or by "me". And this "me" was deeper and more powerful, as it had been when it had asked the voice of fear to go to another chair in my therapist's office for a few minutes.

"I" remained untouched by these sounds, and then realized that I could remain similarly unaffected by my own stories.

A colleague of Michael's, Jim Dreaver, had written a book, which I liked, called, *End Your Story, Begin Your Life*.

It was then that I began to recognize that the entire clamor in my head, which I had always assumed was me, was really a bunch of repetitive stories – or conditioned programs.

I also told Michael about my fatigue and feeling of something "off" every morning, and how it seemed to clear up later in the day. I was distressed that I could not control this discomfort or find a way out of it. Every morning was an intense struggle with my idea of how I should feel.

"What would happen," Michael asked, "if you knew this is how it would be for the rest of your life?"

This gave me pause, and at first I remarked that it would suck. But then, as I reflected, I realized that once I knew for certain that there was nothing to be done, acceptance would be the only option.

Paradoxically this made it "better" and eventually when I gave myself permission to rest and not berate myself for my lack of energy (as Michael also suggested) I found that some mornings were better than others, but that generally, the afternoon and evening were better, and the feelings would pass as night followed day.

I grew to accept whatever the sensations were.

I recognized that "from the inside" this seemed to be how it felt to get older, and the more resistance I felt the worse it became. Allowing the feelings to just "be" what they were provided a sense of tranquility that was new and very soothing.

Then I read *Still Here*, by Ram Dass, and had to confront the fact that what I was experiencing was not avoidable – I would die one day and aging was natural.

Acceptance was not a panacea, but it was very helpful and ultimately, what other option did I have?

Michael and I became friends, and as he was also single we talked about other things, mainly women.

I became aware how my conditioned belief that I could only find happiness through relationship was causing me a lot of suffering, and putting enormous pressure on any possibility of connection.

I also became more deeply aware of my obsessive thoughts about women. On one occasion I had had a conversation with someone in the group prior to one of the meetings and was looking forward to seeing her on the following Saturday.

My mind began to devise strategies around asking her for coffee.

When she arrived that day I was already seated and she did not acknowledge me. I spent the entire meeting wondering what I should do. After the meeting she went up to talk to Michael.

I went out to the car and waited, and I then all of the sudden, started laughing. I suddenly realized that I had missed the entire meeting because of my thoughts about what might or should happen. And further, these thoughts had had no effect upon any potential outcome.

It was like the football game. My inner world in the head had nothing to do with external reality.

I remembered something my ex-girlfriend had said to me – that I wasn't dating her but rather a woman who existed only in my mind.

And it hit me again. How many times had this happened? I was continually wrapped up in my own thoughts and oblivious to the fact that this woman had her own issues, and that's why she was coming to the meeting.

None of it had anything to do with "me". She was completely unaware of my thoughts and intentions, but I had made myself miserable.

As Michael had suggested, my mind was the cause of all of my suffering. I continued to notice how feelings and thoughts about the past and future were affecting my present.

A short while later I shared with the group my apprehension of going to Chicago where I was invited to attend a celebration for my niece's wedding. I was eager to go because I had recently reconnected with her father, and felt like this was my only remaining real family.

But I shared with the group how anxious I was, and described how I was afraid of getting stuck on the plane, dealing with a rental car, missing connections and other potential pitfalls.

Michael looked at me and asked, "Tom, what if you went to Chicago and had a really good time?"

I stopped for a moment and thought and again I burst out laughing. I said, "My God, that was the only thing that had never occurred to me."

My voice of fear was still active and trying to protect me. And look at the price I was paying. I ended up going, and having a wonderful experience.

On the morning I left I cried because I realized that I would meet my nieces for the first time.

3.15

The Allure of Victimhood

One of the benefits of attending the group and reading the work of Eckhart Tolle was becoming familiar with the tricks of the Ego as he describes it. To Eckhart the Ego doesn't care whether you are happy or unhappy; it just wants attention.

The common view of the Ego is that it wants to be Donald Trump and self-aggrandize. A big Ego is considered to be a person who is full of themselves and pumped up on achievement.

But according to Eckhart Tolle, there's another aspect: the function of the Ego is simply to try to become the Self, and be recognized as such.

Again this can be seen with the gambling experience. The emotion of loss is palpable and seemingly negative – but for the Ego the jolt of energy is still addictive.

The Ego, then, serves as a survival program, because it is afraid of its death – and serves to convince you that if its program ends, so do you.

Eckhart says that the Ego can also gain strength and recognition as a victim by spinning its stories of deprivation and unfairness to form a powerful negative identity.

Sometimes this is fueled by an individual or collective "pain body" – a repository of hurt and grievance that is even stored in one's DNA.

Regardless, this negative aspect of the Ego becomes the center of one's conditioned belief system.

When I encountered this theory it resonated deeply with my experience in therapy.

By making space for my feelings and sensing their presence in my body I had identified palpable residues of my parents' experiences during the Holocaust. As I described these to my therapist, I had recognized that they colored my life experience with a darkness that other people did not have.

This became very apparent when I moved to California, where everyone is happy and positive and I found that my dark and negative, fear-based outlook was incomprehensible to many of the people I encountered.

But it was only when I read the concept of Ego as Victim that I realized that how I saw the world and **how I viewed myself in relation to others was a choice**, a choice that had been imprinted mainly by my parents.

I now saw clearly that my programming to please them also made me adopt their worldview and seek confirmation in my experiences; this was true even though, as my therapist had pointed out, my parents would have wanted nothing more than my happiness.

But this crystallization of the Ego as negative was deep and unconscious. In therapy I had managed to get below the surface but it still tended to come up and run my life.

A friend and coach whom I met early on in my work suggested that my path was to "heal the Holocaust"; and when I first heard this I recoiled because I felt deeply that my parents' grievances were real, and that it was my duty to continue to honor them.

This was also the motivation to publish my mother's memoirs – *The Next Chapter* – which is not so much about the Holocaust but rather how difficult it was to adjust to "normal" life after such trauma, and how "normal" people could never comprehend the alienation my mother felt.

I remembered how my therapist had referred to my mother as "a traumatized young woman" during the time we had spent together in Switzerland while waiting for my father to set up things in New York so we could emigrate. I had shared so much of her anguish throughout my mother's life – but these were emotions not shared by others with whom I came into contact.

But after working with my therapist I came to the conclusion that a wonderful way to honor my parents was to lead a rich and productive life in spite of their hardships.

And in fact both of my parents modeled that in retirement; they enjoyed a wonderful seven and 14 years respectively, living near the beach in La Jolla.

Meanwhile I realized that I was carrying on a belief system that they had finally dropped. Both my parents enjoyed their last years enormously.

Slowly but surely I began to experiment with another way. I became friendlier and nicer to people and began to notice how my life experience improved. I allowed my natural generosity, which had been limited only to people whom I trusted in my immediate circle, to extend further outward, and suddenly I began to flourish.

Victimhood tendencies continue to get triggered – but more sporadically. If I see a web post denying the Holocaust I will react – but in an appropriate way.

But going deeper into silence, I could feel what this anger and hatred were doing to my sense of who I was, and with meditation and love it could be refocused.

3.16

Russia Doesn't Exist

One evening I was in a conversation with Michael Jeffreys about the nature of the Self and our belief systems.

Michael was involved in a practice called ***deconstruction*** and he would describe how our consciousness "fills in the blanks" of our perception. For example, if we look at a car on the street from a distance, we take for granted that the part of the car that is hidden from us is still there.

Similarly when we close our eyes we remain confident that the room around us hasn't changed.

But Michael invited me to challenge these assumptions by saying, "Right now, at this moment, Russia doesn't exist. Only this apartment in West L.A. exists right NOW, for you, and if anything Russia is just a thought."

Immediately I wanted to respond with a "Yes, but …" – and I stopped.

In that instant of silence I realized how much of what we believe, and what we perceive, is merely an "overlay" of conceptual truth onto what IS.

I remembered the woman who I had wanted to ask for coffee and how my entire experience of that meeting had been shaped by my inner turmoil and discomfort.

This was a brief introduction to the teaching known as Nondualism or Advaita, which deals only in what we know with certainty: that we exist here and now. Everything else is subject to skepticism.

Of course this is a position as old as the Greeks and a quick rejoinder often is, "But you can't live that way."

But Eckhart Tolle also says that there is plenty of room for the "formative" mind to plan and live "as though" there is a Russia even if we're not physically there. Eckhart's point is that all that exists is the **present moment**; in the present moment you might actually be in Russia, or think about Russia. Similarly we can "plan" for a potential future, but only in the present moment. The actual future will unfold, as it will – and the culmination of our planning will similarly unfold in the present moment in the future.

One of the mind's great functions, in terms of survival, is to "simulate" an If/Then hypothesis – as a programmer might.

And the body will respond as though that was already reality – fear or flight.

But questioning all elements of our perception can serve to expose the true depth of our conditioning and programming.

Michael said that consciousness (like computers) will use the least "processing power" to only reveal the part of reality that is necessary in one's current existence, so in actuality there is "no Russia" while you're not thinking about it (as a thought) or while you're not there physically (as a land mass).

This is the beginning of a shift to an awareness of Consciousness as primary, and it is very powerful, yet it goes against the massive conditioning that has shaped our education and life experience.

This issue was the crux of a famous conversation between Einstein and Tagore – a spiritual teacher and contemporary – who suggested to the physicist that the reason he could not conform quantum mechanics to his other theories was that his own consciousness affected the measurement – Tagore then told Einstein that reality required Einstein's participation.

This may have prompted Einstein's famous quote: "Reality is an illusion, albeit a very persistent one."

At one of our meetings Michael related an experience where he was watching a well-known YouTube video of a young boy singing "*Amazing Grace*"; he described that he was so moved by the performance that tears began streaming down his cheeks.

Then he stopped and said that he realized that his tears were in response to simply the sound from the speakers synchronized with pixels on his monitor.

There was nothing intrinsically sad or moving occurring at that moment other than his own conditioned responses to a series of changes in pixels and sound waves.

Seeing this from this perspective made him realize that EVERYTHING was emanating from within "himself"; he was overlaying the performance with his own conditioned responses.

This suggested to the group that the structure of thought contained NO intrinsic emotional content – rather it was simply "seeing" or "hearing" energy completely devoid of meaning.

Consider the impact on the Ego that is attached to victimhood – it will always seize on such opportunities to go into "the story".

Another way to approach this came up again with Michael in the park. We looked at a tree and talked about its "being".

Michael made me see clearly and deeply that the words we use to describe the "tree" are not the tree itself.

The tree itself is a vibrant living entity in harmony with its environment, and inseparable from the soil, the earth, the sky, the clouds and the planet and the solar system.

The word "tree" is of another level of being. It is a concept.

And the stories around victimhood are similarly merely concepts – to which to give energy or from which to detach.

While the difference between the word "tree" and its reality may be obvious at first, it is a very subtle and significant insight, because we live almost all of our lives in the conceptual reality of our minds.
For example, the actions of another may also be judged from the conceptual prison of "victimhood" as described earlier, and we are convinced that what someone else did is wrong.

The reality can simply be that the other person was unaware of her effect and engrossed in her own world. It was like the woman whose apparent snub had distracted me from an entire session of our group – and whose "snub" was easily reinterpreted as a preoccupation with her own stuff.

This is a matter of "point of view" and in many ways the theory of relativity applies; we each have a unique perspective based on our unique biology and actual physical being. We generally take for granted as "the way things are" until someone or something shows us other ways to perceive life.

But even the visual perspective of another person across the street is completely different.

Recalling the conversation with Michael, they may be seeing one side of the same car or truck for which we "filled in" the other side.

As Tagore suggested to Einstein – no "objective truck" really exists apart from its different apparitions within the consciousness of various observers.
Expanding this out to more subjective thought patterns is very powerful.

So what happens to the concept of "mine" or "ownership"? It turns out to be an arbitrary abstraction.

There are still indigenous people on the earth who don't understand ownership. This was why many Native Americans signed over their land to the U.S. government for next to nothing – their consciousness did not comprehend the notion of "owning" land, which was part of nature.

This can also be seen in our misinterpretation of the Egyptian belief in "Neters" which we have translated as Gods; or apparent superstitious entities they believed in.

Instead, as rogue archeologists have pointed out, Neters represented aspects of the Great Reality of Order in Nature, which the Egyptians called Maat. So a Neter like the Nile Flood irrigated their crops as part of an immensely greater intelligence.

Eckhart Tolle also sees ownership as a result of naming oneself and then gaining "possessions" which are simply labels or purely mental agreements.

In our group Michael pointed out that the concept of ownership probably emerges early as a toddler when one encounters one's name, and is given "things" to identify. It's not a big leap of insight to then begin to identify the self with one's name, and eventually one's possessions.

But over time the sense of "Me" becomes so palpable as to never be questioned. The noticing faculty, which can be termed "awareness", fades into the background and we identify solely with the content of "our" thoughts and Me crystallizes.

But it became clear that practice of questioning every aspect of one's perception is very valuable, and such *deconstruction* served to begin to loosen the hold of conceptual truths that I'd always taken for granted … and which, upon reflection was the cause of my anxiety.

For Westerners our deeply rooted materialist belief system will always convince us that the other side of the car is still "there" – until we look just a bit deeper.

In the computer world this set of assumptions is being shaken by games and virtual reality – because the ability to simulate a reality (like Russia, for example) has become so convincing that someone with a VR (Virtual Reality) headset believes it completely – as we do when we "fill-in" what we believe is the unseen part of the car we see across the street.

It is precisely by beginning to notice just how much of life is "filled in" by our mind, independent of actual experience, that we can open to a new way of seeing – and being.

3.17

Meditation:
A Practice of Observation and Acceptance

Michael introduced the group to other teachers besides Eckhart Tolle, who described how observing the tricks of the mind, is a powerful and important practice.

The key point, however, is that it cannot be done hypothetically using only the intellect. As I had discovered in my therapy sessions, the actual process of making space for all sensations, feelings and thoughts is what creates the gap that allows for transcendence – and it can't be faked.

These other spiritual teachers in the area of Nondualism or Advaita and were effective in deconstructing thought patterns even further.

With this practice all thoughts are no longer identified as "us", but inspected separately and seen as automatically running "subroutines" – or programs.

It is also unusual for these habitual thoughts to be positive. They're generally critical and fear-based.

Michael related his own experience of reading a book one day and noticing a troublesome thought that suddenly arose about a problem. But he stopped and realized that a moment ago everything had been fine, and he said to his mind, "You thought of the problem, you deal with it."

I remembered that Eckhart Tolle also writes about the fact that you can talk to your mind, and even tell it off, which is another indication that your mind isn't all there is to "you".

And this is a powerful tool, as I had learned with my therapist when I had asked my fearful mind to step aside for a moment.

The more frequently this gap occurs, and is noticed, the more detached one becomes.

(Eckhart says, "The mind is a wonderful tool, but a terrible master.")

It is equally important to recognize that this mind can't solve anything by itself, because it is concerned only with two things – the future and the past. And the only time when anything can be accomplished is the present.

The more I observed my "self" as it functioned in the world, the more I saw how my defensiveness and fear had pushed people away and created tension.

For years I had been meditating daily for 15 or 20 minutes in an effort to alleviate my anxiety. But now I came to a completely different understanding of the practice.

Eckhart Tolle says that true presence is not a matter of how long you can sit with your eyes closed. And it is also not a matter of "doing it right".

Actually it is the exact opposite. Sitting quietly or meditating is simply observing the inner programming that judges things as either right or wrong, and allowing it to simply continue without attachment.

During meditation your mind will interrupt "you" with many messages. *Time to go, You itch, Impatience, Resistance, How will I drive to work?*

The realization dawns that none of these "issues" require a response in that moment. They are just programs running the background that are seeking your attention.

To use another computer comparison, they are like popups on the Internet. Each of them tries to announce its importance, but if we look deeply we begin to develop a faculty, that with practice, can simply let these "programs" run their course.

And Life continues.

At one point during meditation I noticed that the fearful voice in the head was actually an excellent planner. I had caught my "self" mapping out a route for my errands.

I complimented my "planning mind" on its ability to solve potential problems but asked it to wait until those problems actualized to reassert itself. Or just wait until later.

In the Gurdjieff teaching this practice is seen as a struggle against unseen forces.

"We undertake the struggle to be vigilant, to watch – the struggle of the watchman. We seek to have a watchman in us who is stable. The one who watches is the one who is present."

– Jeanne de Salzmann (Longtime student of Gurdjieff and tasked with continuing his work upon his death)

But we often find that if we do struggle with our mind ("mentally") it gives it energy.

Experimenting with specific responses that go against habit can be powerful. Noticing the effort to shave with the left hand (if right-handed) shows the power of habits grooved into our brains. Or consciously deciding not to answer a phone call or text right away brings a feeling of inner power and spaciousness.

Letting things go, more and more, shows us that very little that the mind comes up with is really urgent. And this mode of acceptance and surrender, paradoxically, leads to a powerful new calm source of energy and confidence.

Another insight that becomes apparent during such quiet periods, particularly in nature, is how extraneous "you" are to most of the processes of life. At first, this can be unsettling to notice.

The brook will keep babbling, the birds will keep singing, "you" will keep breathing, sweating, stretching, walking, and so on with or without "your" direct participation.

Even your death is just such an idea, for now. It is a hypothetical that can and will cause anxiety when it becomes a focal point for attention.

In some ways this may be what Gurdjieff referred to as "the terror of the situation", and it can be frightening to consider.

Especially for the Ego, its very existence and idea of "you" or "I" is the most important thing in the world.

But during quiet periods or meditation, the apparent irrelevance of the Ego's clamor for attention can expose it for the phantom that it is. When those conceptual imperatives fall away all that is left is awareness or consciousness.

Of course at first this is a very disturbing notion on many levels, and the Ego will literally fight for its life. As awareness grows, one begins to notice the many tricks of what Buddhism calls the "monkey-mind".

Familiar patterns begin to emerge which trigger the defenses of the Ego, such as feeling slighted, inadequate, rejected and so on. Each of these experiences strengthens the identity of the Ego as victim.

But ultimately the discovery of the phantom nature of the "I" thought can be very liberating. If there is no You, as some sages have suggested, who is there to be lonely, anxious, a failure, or the container for any other judgment.

Michael described his own inquiry where he tried to find him-"self" in his body. First he could recognize that he wasn't his thoughts or his emotions but something was still apparently "there" as "him".

Finally he identified the sensation of himself as just a persistent feeling in his chest. So was HE that feeling?

How could he be? HE was the one that had noticed it. And then HE noticed that HE was apparently the one who noticed "the thought" that named the sensation …

With this sort of inquiry the false-self can be eventually uncovered and exposed as a phantom.

But what about personal responsibility? Modern neuroscience, and David Eagleman in particular, have raised many legal issues about the consequences of not being able to find a single, solid stable "you" to take responsibility.

But perhaps there is a balance, not in our analytical ways of determining what is "right" – but rather after allowing some space and some love to enter "we" do know what to do and what not to do.

Without a "you" do try to control everything; paradoxically a higher intelligence and deeper knowing can emerge.

The reality that I discovered with my cat is that when you become a bit "sane" by trusting life and being present, the notion of hurting anyone or anything becomes a non-issue.

And as Michael Jeffreys says, "Would you rather be right, or happy?"

Noticing and pausing this impulse to justify, and to be "right" creates another space that lets us begin to let go of many things which we deemed very significant.

Beginning to deeply notice what is, with or without your mental judgment or participation, right here and now, can lead to amazing realizations. It is a powerful practice.

Let it be.

3.18

Doing the Opposite: Leaving the Comfort Zone

As I discovered in therapy, we have assumptions about others and ourselves that can evaporate under closer scrutiny.

Because our brain can also seem to "malfunction," I've been keenly interested in what neuroscientists believe about our nature, and seen how it resonates with my experience.

In some ways, as a computer guy, I was looking for the "user manual" for my mind.

One of the first books I turned to was *Evolve Your Brain: The Science of Changing Your Mind*, by Joe Dispenza. Dispenza was featured in the movie *What the Bleep Do We Know!?* Like many neuroscientists, Dispenza shows how deeply conditioning first affects our beliefs and then our outlook – and ultimately our reality – and how so much of what we think of as "us" is merely habitual, repetitive programming.

I remember on one occasion when I was particularly anxious I tried to just sit quietly for 20 minutes to see what would happen. My laptop was right next to me on a small table and without thinking (without "me") my hand reached out and grabbed the mouse to check email.

I was shocked. "Who" was checking email?

Dispenza does believe in the ability or volition of the human being to change bad habits – whether into "other habits" or through what one might call free choice – by reprogramming the mind as one might a computer.

Dispenza's most compelling example involved a depressed patient where he did what George Costanza once did on an episode of *Seinfeld;* he consciously "did the opposite" of what he would ordinarily do. At a coffee shop when George saw a beautiful woman, instead of remaining awkwardly silent, he went up to her and told her he was unemployed, living at home and she responded positively – something he never anticipated.

This may or may not work in "real life" but Dispenza describes how such reprogramming can occur when the observer "decides" to take chances (as I did when adopting my cat) and how such new experiences reprogram perceptions. According to Dispenza, in such instances where one leaves a "comfort zone" the brain actually forges new connections via new neural networks, thereby bypassing the "time worn grooves" of habitual automatic responses and creating now potential programs.

In some ways it's like downloading a file or an entirely new operating system. In neuroscience it is called "neuroplasticity" – the ability of the brain to "learn" new patterns by reshaping its own neural networks.

Doing something new and uncomfortable can also tap a reserve of energy – one we never knew we had.

Anthony Robbins also talks about "taking action" to reprogram one's habitual negative beliefs, which Robbins also refers to as an inner mental "technology".

But this brings us back to "who am I" really? Who is the "one" that first can notice this conditioning and even make choices in order to change it? From somewhere, seemingly "inside the brain" but perhaps from another source, this mysterious energy emerges seemingly on its own.

In *I Am a Strange Loop*, Douglas Richard Hofstadter also follows a mathematical and computer model to dig down into where and what the individual "Self" may be.

As a mathematician, neuroscientist and philosopher Hofstadter begins with the primacy of number.

This is because whatever symbols we use to represent "numbers", the logical relationships that follow adhere to certain logical truths. This resonates with the parallels between DNA and computer code – all code is a symbolic representation that can be "decoded" for its inherent logical and structural reality.

As we saw earlier, a wonderful linguistic and logical paradox is expressed in: "The sentence 'This sentence has ten words' has ten words." - (*I Am a Strange Loop*)

Since the underlying sentence has ten words it seems to be true but upon "reflection" its "truth" is paradoxical because the "inner sentence" has only four words.

So where is truth to be found?

To Hofstadter this paradoxical aspect of language is an obvious manifestation of the inevitable abstraction that results from mind – which only simulates nature or reality.

Absurd contradictions like this suggest that no words or concepts can truly "explain" reality.

As Hofstadter suggests a "truer" representation of nature is mathematical – like the Fibonacci sequence (an infinite sequence of numbers) or a constant like Pi, which is ALWAYS TRUE in terms of the relationship within a geometric shape (the circle, where the radius is in a specific relationship to the circumference).

Another illustration of a loop can be found if we look once more at computer programming.

How does a computer count? Generally it names a variable ("i") and then begins to set conditions for i + 1 and program the loop to continue for "each i" until another condition is met.

All such looping programs (or subroutines) proceed (if there are no bugs) completely logically.

And the logic must be an inherent "function" of the programming language – suggesting once again the mysterious origin of the inner consistency of our genetic programming or DNA.

But describing them verbally will not allow us to debug the program. Programmers will put comments in quotes or separated by commas to explain their thinking to others but the truth only emerges *in running the program*.

The verb is where the truth is.

As Hofstadter points out, language can only explain characteristics. This reminds me of the famous statement by Krishnamurti that once we identify a bird by its name we cease seeing it forever.

Our current science is mostly labels. It is virtually devoid of depth and understanding.

Thought, like our inner "I," is looped and imperfect – with the inherent limitation of needing to be expressed through language.
Nondual teacher Rupert Spira points out that in English the subject-object structure of each sentence leads to an underlying assumption of separation. "I am hungry," posits an "I" that exists separately from the world that may nourish it.

Alan Watts poses the question – when one says, "It is raining" – who exactly is "It"?

Taking reality as one absolute Whole, however, it is our language that inadequately describes life (a totality of perfection, infinity mathematical certainty; number) in a way that is limited to what our finite minds can comprehend – as fragmented, imperfect analogies to reality.

Hofstadter goes on to argue that the only way to comprehend consciousness is through "story" – or by analogy –and just as the linguistic descriptions of mathematical absolutes fall short, so too does story or analogy never completely "explain" or "describe" the true "nature" of consciousness.

By taking this one aspect of language as the pointer to reality and meaning – *analogy*; or "metaphor" -- this is actually another metaphor for the relationship between hardware to software.

Software or consciousness – unlike hardware or the brain – is "no thing." It is pure energetic activity and a reflection of an immense infinite intelligence.

Hofstadter contends that as systems evolve, for example cells organized into organs like the heart and eventually the brain, when feedback loops manifest as "selves" – at this point organic molecules become animate or "alive." He still assumes, however, that such organization occurs randomly.

But keep in mind that nature's patterns can be decoded mathematically- like the Fibonacci sequence or sequenced DNA.

But let's look again at the specific instance of a loop, "Next i" in computer programming – where the variable "I" (pun intended) takes on additional values as the program executes.

"In a loop structure, the program asks a question, and if the answer requires an action, it's performed and the original question is asked again until the answer is such that the action is no longer required. For example, a program written to compute a company's weekly payroll for each individual employee will begin by computing the wages of one employee and continue performing that action in a loop until there are no more employee wages to be computed, and only then will the program move on to its next action. Each pass through the loop is called an "iteration". Loops constitute one of the most basic and powerful programming concepts."

– Webopedia: http://www.webopedia.com/TERM/L/loop.html

Both our minds and computers apparently operate in this way to calculate hypothetical potential outcomes.

Like If/Then, our minds may run "What If" loops indefinitely unless stopped (be presence).

So now, once again, we can ask the original question – where did the Intelligence come from to discover, if not originally write, manifest or "compile" the organic programming language that is DNA?

How could such intelligence or consciousness arise or emanate from an inanimate object – how are the qualia or the experiences of consciousness somehow an "emergent" property of seemingly inanimate neurons?

Could it happen by chance, from a lightning bolt hitting a swamp? Remember Fred Hoyle's analogy of the tornado in a junkyard. That seems infinitely unlikely.

3.19

There's Someone in My Head ... and It's Not Me

Pink Floyd sang, "There's someone in my head and it's not me." This line is quoted in the beginning of *Incognito: The Secret Life of the Brain* by neuroscientist David Eagleman.

Eagleman in many ways echoes the work of Eckhart Tolle when he points to the latest brain research suggesting that there is not one part of the physical self that contains the "I".

He explains that the brain is such a complex entity that its many networks are like a "democracy of committees" which coordinate behavior by consensus and make choices in ways we don't fully understand.

Like others in his field, Eagleman, can't locate a single physical area of the brain that is "in charge." And he compares the various networks of the brain and their "subroutines" (patterns of conditioned behavior) to political parties. The networks "consult" and coordinate in a manner that ultimately lead to choices and behaviors based on conflict and eventual compromise. Eagleman writes:

"But we do not find parts of the brain that is not itself driven by other parts of the network. Instead every part of the brain is densely connected with – and driven by – other brain parts. And that suggests that no part is independent and therefore 'free.'"

– *Incognito*, page 166

Eagleman uses examples of people with impaired or injured brains and also celebrities like Mel Gibson, who was "not himself" when drunk, turned into a raging anti-Semite, and was conciliatory when sober.

One area where this has far reaching ramifications is the law, and Eagleman suggests a legal system based not on blame, which he considers an outmoded concept, but rather on the prospects for modifiability. Eagleman believes that if we can reasonably surmise that a criminal will not repeat (act of passion) or can be rehabilitated (behavior modified) then reprogramming is the preferred result; if the behavior is chronic Eagelman agrees that the person must be separated from society.

Eagleman compares the achievements in neuroscience to those in astronomy, who challenged conventional beliefs about the earth as the center of the universe – in the case of the brain the notion of the single responsible and cohesive Self is exposed as a vast oversimplification.

In *Incognito*, he concludes,

"In the same way that the Cosmos is much larger than we ever imagined, we ourselves are something greater than we had intuited by introspection. We're now getting the first glimpse of the vastness of inner space ... What a perplexing masterpiece the brain is, and how lucky we are to be in a generation that has the technology and the will to turn our attention to it. It is the most wondrous thing in the universe, and it is us."

I find this language both inspiring and a bit daunting – it is always humbling to confront the reality of the vastness of what we don't know – and in fact may never know.

Eagleman says that in the traditional view of perception is that information from the outside world pours into the senses, works its way through the brain, and makes itself consciously seen, heard and felt.

But it is interesting to consider that within this modern view of neuroscience, with no finite "I" to be located, that our "inner space" can be described as infinite as the Cosmos.

And many scientists are coming to think that sensory input may merely revise ongoing internal activity in the brain – and that there is a vast inner life going on of which we are largely unconscious.

If we think about how our bodies operate – as Eckhart Tolle describes the "immense intelligence" of our unconscious functions – which regulates breath, respiration, and so on is very much like a computer operating system that "runs" even when no program is loaded (or "active").

Something is always happening. The clock on our phone or PC never stops. It is "active" even while just "waiting" for input. The encoded intelligence is active even when the computer is passive.

And Eagleman notes, sensory input is superfluous for perception: when our eyes are closed during dreaming, we can still enjoy a rich and visual experience. From an information processing perspective, the awake state may be essentially the same as the dreaming state, only apparently influenced by "external" stimuli. From this perspective, our apparent conscious life is merely an awake dream.

So perhaps even when we're not using it, the phone or brain is dreaming, as Philip K. Dick suggested in the book that inspired the movie *Blade Runner – Do Androids Dream of Electric Sheep?* But we are not androids; **the operating system we are running is organic.**

Remember too that within the biochemistry of the brain, our thoughts and dreams are electrical signals between synapses, recorded and perceived by networks of billions of neurons.

And this also means, of course, that our entire notion of the smooth passage of time and space is merely a construction of the brain.

Recall the words of Rupert Spira: "Just as thought makes pure Consciousness appear as time, so perception makes pure Consciousness appear as space."

Just as our minds "create" or "fill-in" the other side of the truck that we see across the street, so too have we innately learned and accepted the "reality" of time and space.

This resonates with many spiritual traditions and the entire notion of awakening ...

Perhaps awakening is a "re-cognition" of the true relationship of one's tiny "self" to the vast Self of which the brain is tuned into.

(You can find out more about Eagleman in his article for Discover: *Ten Mysteries of the Brain* and his PBS series on *The Brain*.)

What these scientific findings about the brain suggest is that the "self" is a temporary program, or set of programs that run on their own. Gurdjieff's work suggests that a controlling faculty can emerge, but the question will always follow: Who is that?

As Eagleman suggests, a true Copernican-like revolution may be needed to render the entire question irrelevant.

Instead of localizing consciousness in the brain, the nonlocality concepts of quantum physics may lead to an entirely different conclusion; perhaps conscious awareness is part of a "decentralized" intelligence that remains as elusive to our knowledge as actual center of our solar system was to our ancestors, only to be replaced by a series of new "centers" in the vastness of the Cosmos.

In his book *Self Comes to Mind*, neuroscientist Antonio Damasio states that this miraculous harmonious brain activity which results in a sense of self emerges for evolutionary reasons – for the same reason that a microbe will gravitate toward nourishment and away from toxins – for "homeostasis" or basically to maintain its being. Life is programmed to survive.

(This again resonates with the work of Eckhart Tolle, who when asked about why the Ego arose if it creates suffering, replied that it was an evolutionary arising – a step within vast cosmic processes.)

With the evolution of human brains, our affinity toward pleasure and away from pain is merely far more complex by using complex inner mental simulations.

Damasio asserts that the relatively "new" concept of a Self may have resulted from interbreeding with other humanoids, forming one new complete extremely complex system forming the Mind/Body or what we now call "man".

Just as Eagleman talked about the various neural networks as political parties, Damasio sees the "Autobiographical Self" as the conductor of a symphony that does not exist until the orchestra begins to play [harmoniously].

Of course if there is disharmony, then we have a malfunction – or in computer terms – a conflict between programs.

This potential for harmony and "orchestration" of neural systems is the result of the underlying nature of life itself – Damasio writes:

"Managing and safekeeping life is the fundamental premise of biological value." (*Self Comes to Mind*, page 25)

"[Self] Consciousness came into being because of biological value, as contributor to more effective value management. [Natural selection] But consciousness did not invent biological value or the process of valuation. Eventually, in human minds, consciousness revealed biological value and allowed the development of new ways and means of managing it." (*Self Comes to Mind*, page 28)

"Consciousness" here is used to refer to a sense of a separate self – not in the universal sense.

In other words, who we are is a tiny part of a far higher intelligence (that preceded the development of our own brains) enabling us finally to notice our "selves" and begin to comprehend a sliver of reality, all for our continued survival?

If we consider that our known software programs are also created with intention; that is, to create and edit a document or graphics, it is interesting to posit that a similar "intention" of an evolutionary "program" would be its own survival.

This resonates with Dr. Robert Lanza's theory of "Biocentrism" or biological relativity because whatever a conceptual self may be, it would necessarily result from a life form's sensory capacity and biology.

One might then wonder what sense of "self" a whale or dolphin may have with a larger brain than our own, in a "world" created by sound and a vast ocean in which to live and play.

We know that our pets, dogs and cats, respond to stimuli we cannot hear or smell. This speaks to the limited understanding we have of the entire electromagnetic spectrum, where even with our most sensitive instruments we can only "perceive" a tiny fraction of the energy in our universe.
So then who are "we" individually?

Basically we are a collection of stories that come together out of experiences formed electrically through the firing of neural networks and stored in the soft tissue of the brain's "hard drives" or what we call memory.

According to neuroscientists like Damasio, the Self "emerges" from a level of cognitive complexity that yields consciousness – similar to the critical mass attained in a computer network – such as the Internet.

However, even though Damasio maintains that the concept of the self is an emerging function of neural networks, neuroscience is still at a loss to explain consciousness (the qualia or experience of awareness and all other perceptions) can arise from inanimate matter.

As Eagleman suggests, just as our egocentric cosmology of the earth being the center of the universe has now given way to the reality that we exist on the periphery of an average galaxy literally in the middle of nowhere; so too we may need to come to terms with the fact that what we deem to be us, and what we think is "conscious," is a mere tip of an enormous iceberg of (ephemeral and nonlocal) consciousness.

The next "Copernican Revolution" may actually be prompted by our deep and profound recognition that our brain (and body) is epigenetically a receiver of higher energies, and that "we" as labels are simply illusory and arbitrary.

This perception of a true relationship of our conceptual identity to a far greater Being/Mind is very likely the necessary next stage of discovery for what we consider to be science.

But what can our current limited science point us to? What might a new science yield?

3.20

Being the Scientist

Michael Jeffreys used to suggest that one not try to control one's life or its circumstances, but instead investigate and experiment without prejudgment – to be "the scientist".

(This was suggested as a way of counterbalancing the victimhood programs that can make us prejudge situations and coalesce within ourselves as a feeling of lack.)

Modern science does generally proceed from a "hypothesis" which it attempts to prove or disprove, and which can also skew the outcome in favor what the scientist expects or desire.

Unlike this current "politicized science" practiced in business and universities, what Michael suggests is more like a "Sacred Science" that is open to truth beyond and apart from our preconceptions.

Shifting our attitude in this manner can produce interesting results. In many ways it is aligned with Joe Dispenza's notion of going beyond our comfort zone to create new neural networks or memory grooves.

And, actually being such a "scientist" will serve to experientially disprove the prevailing attitude, or "programming," that suggests that allowing things to unfold and simply observing them will lead to passivity or apathy.

In our group it would often happen that someone would say, "This is all well and good but if I become accepting (and open) then all I will do is sit around on my couch and do nothing."

This is a hypothesis of the egoic mind, which thrives on activity and craves attention.

The response from Michael was – "Try it and see."

(In some ways this is also reminiscent of nondual teacher Wayne Liquorman's suggestion about free will – if you think you have it, use it.)

The reality is that life has its own agenda and we will still do things (according to our nature).

There is no pause button. The clock in the computer keeps on ticking. It's an endless loop.

And as Eckhart Tolle writes, there are periods of extreme activity and then there are periods of relaxation and inactivity. Our egoic minds dislike "not doing" because it removes attention from the voice in the head.

The conditioned mind likes to stay busy by judging and receiving the attention of awareness, rather than allowing awareness (and life) to simply be what it is.

And when this compulsion to control and judge reaches its limit, we crash.

Conceptual Hell

- I'm Smart
- I'm Good
- I'm Enlightened
- I'm Loved
- I'm Successful

- I'm Stupid
- I'm Bad
- I'm Insane
- I'm Lonely
- I'm Worthless

Life

I finally put this to the test through direct experimentation.

I had a busy afternoon ahead; I wanted to get my car serviced, hit the market and dry cleaner and try to accomplish a few other tasks before evening rush hour.

Previously I would have allowed my mind to race ahead with thoughts of, "If I can get the oil change done in less than an hour, then etc. etc." As with my trip to Chicago, making advance plans and then evaluating the way that Life met my expectations resulted in a set of judgments.

On this occasion I determined to embark on the errands with no preconceived notions of how they should unfold. I decided that I would allow each experience to happen and adapt if necessary.

In fact, the oil change turned into a situation where I had to bring the car back after I noticed something was wrong with my lights. But instead of stressing (and creating a story) about it, I asked the mechanic to please fix it and he took care of it without a fuss.

It reminded me of Eckhart Tolle's story about getting a bowl of cold soup at a restaurant and either complaining, "How dare you serve me cold soup" or matter of factly asking that it be reheated.

By not making it into a problem and taking it as an affront to a false "me", the energy around the situation remained stable and things worked out. Keeping my (aggrieved) self out of it made everything less stressful and Life seemed to take care of it.

Similarly at the dry cleaner and market, I noticed my initial annoyance that there was a short line, and allowed for other customers to be in front of me.

Then, in the Express Lane at the market, when someone had to pay by check, instead of fuming I let it happen while I read a magazine.

When I got home, a bit later than anticipated, instead of being a bundle of nerves, I was strangely relaxed.

This is not always possible. As Michael also says, "When you are caught up in the madness, it is hard to 'shut down the program'".

Many of our most deeply conditioned programs, like the voice of fear, have a power and life of their own. The most significant discovery we can make, however, is that none of them are truly "you".

What are you? As Eckhart Tolle says, you are "no thing" – the space in which it all unfolds, and the faculty that is aware of what is happening.

Once the watcher identifies with a thought "he" disappears, and awareness is hijacked by the habitually conditioned mind.

From reading Eckhart Tolle, I have learned so much – first to watch my thoughts and not necessarily to attach importance to any one or set of thoughts.

Second to not take my "self" very seriously and to also observe the different ways my "self" actually interacts with the world (as opposed to how I imagine my "self" to be).

Perhaps most important, if I am able, I can generally remind myself that the present moment – Now – is the only reality – as opposed to my mental fantasies of how things "should" be.

And in any moment, as Eckhart tell us, we have three choices:

- Change the situation;
- Accept the situation;
- Leave the situation.

This practice has enabled me to make the best of many situations where previously I would have stewed, complained and made others and myself miserable.

The practice of allowing outcomes and the acceptance of not knowing creates more spacious circumstances without preconceptions or "hypotheses". Of course this still begs the question of exactly "who" effects a change, accepts or leaves

3.21

Living the Mystery

If we think in terms of the evolution of software, as we currently know it, we find that supercomputers like IBM's Watson can calculate and search at incredible speeds.

Energetically these machines are processing instructions written by humans, mechanistically, using electronics and silicon. Quantum computers and nanotechnology may eventually serve us with greater processing power.

But the operating system and programming language of IBM Watson is not organic; it is qualitatively different from our biology in ways that science has identified.

Within ourselves we have now discovered a similarly programmed harmonious system of intelligently managed energy that we did not design (DNA). This organic or bioplasmic system has evolved over millions of years within a universe that continues to reveal itself as functioning as an even greater system information transfer and exchange of energy.

Our human endeavors and in fact our very being is not isolated, but rather occur ALWAYS AND EVERYWHERE in relationship (Epigenetics) with this informational environment.

And our latest forays into quantum physics confirm that in no way are we somehow objectively separate from the universe or from life; we are in fact Life itself – energetic being, a verb or active intelligence.

This may be what Deepak Chopra means when he says that, *"Your body is a metaphor for experiencing reality."*

We are conditioned to believe that the human body is a physical "thing" that lives for a while and then apparently expires. Our bodies are considered to be a purely material apparatus through which life is lived; so how is it a metaphor?

A metaphor, like the word "God" is a 'variable' or conveyance of meaning.

Once we consider the undeniable presence of awareness as a property of our organic being, there is suddenly a new means through which to interpret the vast field of information in which we live.

As there can be no meaning without Mind, we must posit a Mind at the heart of existence.

And bear "in mind" that Mind is literally "no thing."

With organic DNA and our own software informing silicon, there is an immensely intelligent order by which encoded intelligence operates – it is based on the higher mathematical logic we find in the Fibonacci sequence, the Geometry of the Greeks and Egyptians and now in our own software algorithms that operate across our recently evolved planetary nervous system – the Internet.

And as geneticist Juan Enriquez described in his video, changing the code changes everything.

Therefore the genetic code has meaning. It conveys information. Just as our software is legally considered "intellectual property" in the case of computer code from Microsoft®, Apple® or Google®, it is time to manifest reverence for what we have discovered in nature as undeniable infinite Intelligence.

Beyond the limiting labels of modern science we can now begin to fathom the obvious infinite expression of meaning in all of life.

Just as we cannot debug computer code unless we "run" it – we cannot fathom life without living it.

On our planet we can see this immense connected Intelligence everywhere in the diversity with which life flourishes. Elsewhere we can only try to imagine how life might unfold when it is not limited to being "life as we know it".

Returning to our initial premise that there cannot be information without Mind, we can now go even further as we decode the informational content of the natural universe.

Whether as a "computer simulation" or whatever its ultimate reality might be, we can perhaps begin to recognize that it in our brief tenure as "selves" we are truly conveyances of meaning – living metaphors.

But our current belief system assumes that the scientist can stand apart, objectively studying and understanding nature independent of the observer's participation in its infinite processes.

As Deepak Chopra and others remind us, quantum physics and neuroscience have exposed the myopia of such a science. With all of its achievements in illusory control, modern science has become "Scientism" – a dogma of false separation.

All of our "silo" sciences – biology, neuroscience, astronomy and physics, each within their own narrow endeavors, have reached their apparent limits in the quest for an objective perspective because all measurement is made through the lens of the metaphor—the human being.

In order to live the metaphor we cannot imagine ourselves as any "thing" – we must be a verb. We are what we experience ourselves to be – living awareness or consciousness.

We have seen, what Eckhart calls the Ego is the conditioned seeking mechanism or energy for survival that is comprised of layers of "psychological realities" intertwined as we grow older and keep searching for answers.

When we see that this programmed seeking energy is not "you", and gradually allow it to just be there, there is spaciousness that then creates a vast opening for the true energies of Life to unfold in place of this false self.

This can lead to breakthroughs and more of what the world calls success or just an inner sense of deep fulfillment - but without this realization we're stuck in the quagmire of continuing to look outside at the external world for fulfillment, or to your repetitive inner stories for answers.

Freeing oneself of this false sense of self is what is sometimes called liberation or awakening.

This mechanically programmed thought is not a program to be "uninstalled" but only to be observed dispassionately. Through a practice of consistent observation and non-attachment, the true operating system of the universe – conscious awareness – will gradually dissipate and replace the false operating system of the mechanical, conditioned "self".

There is no "final aha moment" or ultimate ending. It is a continuous process to be experienced moment-to-moment.

And there are useful reminders to increase the gaps between automatic reactions and thoughts.

In a conversation with a Gurdjieff practitioner he noticed my momentary inattention and said, "Try to maintain an inner connection to the sensation of your right arm as we speak."

Others suggest maintaining a conscious connection between the bottoms of our feet and the earth – remaining literally grounded – as we navigate through life.

And Eckhart Tolle suggests either walking through nature silently, or quietly feeling the alive sensation in our hands will foster a sense of stillness that aligns us with Consciousness.

We merge with Awareness and the vast intelligence of Nature – as opposed to continuing mechanically as a separate delusional entity.

All of this is meaningless when considered hypothetically. However, in actual practice, it is powerful.

When consciously remembered and implemented these practices can create a gap in the automatic functioning of our inner computer as it tries to usurp control as "you".

Connecting with this new emergent faculty will draw us deeper toward wholeness and away from the programmed obsessions of seeking, labeling and description that lead to separation and alienation.

Philosopher, Jacob Needleman, ends his masterpiece, *"A Sense of the Cosmos"* by observing:

"To acquire power, the modern age turned to the mechanism of **thought** rather than to **consciousness**. As a result the emotions – unharmonized, untouched by the ideas of the intellect – unconsciously continued their work of governing the life of man under the formation of egoism. Ideas which could have guided the harmonization of mind, feeling and instinct became instead mere explanations which divide and analyze, and through which unity can never be obtained."

The allure of our current science is precisely its apparent ability to control nature based upon a purely intellectual understanding. *"I think therefore I am."*

– Descartes

But as we have discovered through our **very recent** experience with technology and its ubiquity within our biological systems, this sense of power and control is illusory.

We can reprogram, edit, combine and label DNA but a deep, heartfelt and honest connection to its source is nonexistent in our current scientific arenas.

As Needleman says, our current science is a set of labels that remains detached from true Being. Earlier in *A Sense of the Cosmos* he describes a scene where a surgeon is discussing an aspect of anatomy and says with typical arrogance, "Nature got it wrong."

This is reflected currently when we decode DNA whose functions remain unknown and call them "junk".

This is precisely the arrogance of a people who have reprogrammed Life but not comprehended its essential truth – that it is a reflection of an immensely higher Intelligence with which we must align, but which we can never fully comprehend nor control using our conditioned thought systems.

How are we to attain to the unity or sense of connection to which Needleman points?

Can we reprogram ourselves toward perhaps a truly Sacred Science?

In the first chapter of "*A New Earth*", Eckhart Tolle describes how for millions of years lily pads existed as leafy plants in water pools. Then one day, the first flower bloomed as what we label a "lotus", but it was really an expression of a different, perhaps higher frequency, of the source code of DNA. It conveyed a different level (perhaps dimension) of meaning.

Our science might "explain" this as a mutation but it has no explanation for the apparent mental component behind it – the actual evolutionary program or software that suddenly "flowered".

Is the flower more adaptable to sunlight so that it became "naturally selected"? Perhaps but this is another conceptual explanation that we make now – millions of years after the fact.

When Eckhart was asked if the Ego is such a source of suffering, why does it exist? He called it an evolutionary development in humans – in much the same way that the lotus was an evolutionary arising in plants.

And the reality seems to be that our ability to "reason" using thoughts and language has enabled us to survive and even thrive where other species have gone extinct.

But as I saw within my recognition of my own "voice of fear", our reason and thoughts are not truly us but rather, as in computer terms, a "property" or "method" of our true nature.

In programming any object has properties (colors for example which we saw were expressed in RGB values in a macro or web page) and methods (potentialities defined by its nature/code).

But none of these account for experience, or what biologists refer to as qualia – how things feel.

Epigenetics now reveals to us that the code in our cells acts in harmony with the environment, exchanging energy, with our skin, brain and internal organs as harmonious intermediaries.

Our body (as Deepak Chopra suggests) is not figuratively but literally a metaphor or conveyance of such experience.

In *Super Genes*, Deepak and his co-author Rudy Tanzi describe the complexity of the *microbiome* – the community of millions of organisms that inhabit our digestive system and whose genomes influence, and are influenced by our own genes.

"For every one human gene we have, there are 100 associated genes within our microbiome. More than 100 trillion microorganisms live in our gut, mouth, skin and other mucosal surfaces of our bodies. These microbes have numerous beneficial functions relevant to supporting life such as digesting food, preventing disease-causing pathogens from invading the body, and synthesizing essential nutrients and vitamins."

– SecondGenome.com

So that now, beyond our own genes and their interaction with the environmental energies, millions of other genetically diverse entities also interact within "us".

If we've ever felt something "deep in our gut", what is really happening is our experience (qualia) being influenced not just by "our" brain or mind, or emotions, but rather by sensations that are result of millions of biochemical interactions.

How this nonstop frenetic activity allows us to feel *anything* remains a mystery. Science has decoded the programs but how they translate into our mysterious sense of "I Am" is still unknown.

As Jacob Needleman writes in *A Sense of the Cosmos*, it remains a mystery beyond our logical comprehension, both how experience can arise from apparently inanimate matter and how billions of galaxies can exist in "space" without apparent boundaries or end.

The key seems to be the deep and continuing recognition that the metaphor (our "self") and the software (the Mind or DNA) are in no ways separate from anything or everything else.

Just as there is no "outside" when one looks up at the stars, and that "fact" lands like a hammer in our gut when we look up at night – so too is there no scientific or objective knowledge possible – apart or outside of either our "selves" or "what is".

Science, DNA, software, thought and any concept of "God" are all part of the mystery – the entire soup of life – and its "purpose" (if any) is to experience it fully and deeply.

Everything we know, feel and learn takes place in the immediate execution of programs within a vast informational field that we can now see is not only complex, but also cognizant and infinitely intelligent.

Our DNA is intelligently programmed – the intentional meaning of reality itself, manifesting in the fulfillment of its infinite potential.

Glossary of Terms

(Unless otherwise noted, all definitions were retrieved from Wikipedia)

- **> and <**: the "greater-than" symbol, and the "less-than" symbol, are used in various operations that usually pertain to work being done mathematically or with a programming language.

    Example: "A > B" means A is greater than B

- **Algorithm**: a self-contained step-by-step set of operations to be performed.

- **BDSM**: bondage, discipline or dominance, sadism or submission, masochism.

- **Biocentrism**: a concept proposed in 2007 by American doctor of medicine Robert Lanza, which sees biology as the central driving science in the universe.

- **Biomimicry or Biomimetics**: the imitation of the models, systems, and elements of nature for the purpose of solving complex human problems.

- **Creationism**: the religious belief that the Universe and life originated from specific acts of divine creation.

- **Deism**: the belief that God has created the universe but remains apart from it and permits his creation to administer itself through natural laws. Deism thus rejects the supernatural aspects of religion, such as belief in revelation in the Bible, and stresses the importance of ethical conduct.

    http://www.theopedia.com/deism

- **DNA**: Deoxyribonucleic acid, a molecule that carries most of the genetic instructions used in the growth, development, functioning and reproduction of all known living organisms and many viruses.

- **Epigenetics**: the study of heritable changes in gene expression (active versus inactive genes) that does not involve changes to the underlying DNA sequence – a change in phenotype without a change in genotype – which in turn affects how cells read the genes.

  http://www.whatisepigenetics.com/fundamentals

- **Equanimity**: a state of psychological stability and composure which is undisturbed by experience of or exposure to emotions, pain, or other phenomena that may cause others to lose the balance of their mind.

- **Exascale**: computing systems capable of at least one exaFLOPS, or a billion billion calculations per second.

- **Fibonacci Sequence**: a series of numbers in which each number is the sum of the two preceding numbers. The simplest is the series 1, 1, 2, 3, 5, 8, etc.

- **Fundamentalism**: usually has a religious connotation that indicates unwavering attachment to a set of irreducible beliefs. However, fundamentalism has come to apply to a tendency among certain groups – mainly, though not exclusively, in religion – that is characterized by a markedly strict literalism as applied to certain specific scriptures, dogmas, or ideologies, and a strong sense of the importance of maintaining ingroup and outgroup distinctions, leading to an emphasis on purity and the desire to return to a previous ideal from which advocates believe members have strayed. Rejection of diversity of opinion as applied to these established "fundamentals" and their accepted interpretation within the group is often the result of this tendency.

- **Golden Ratio**: represented by Greek letter Phi (Ø). In mathematics two quantities are in the golden ratio if their ratio is the same as the ratio of their sum to the larger of the two quantities.

- **HTML or HyperText Markup Language**: commonly abbreviated as HTML, is the standard markup language used to create web pages.

- **Kabbalah**: Hebrew: קַבָּלָה, "receiving/tradition", is an esoteric method, discipline, and school of thought that originated in Judaism. A traditional Kabbalist in Judaism is called a Mekubbal (Hebrew: מְקוּבָּל).

- **Meditation**: a practice where an individual trains the mind or induces a mode of consciousness, either to realize some benefit or for the mind to simply acknowledge its content without becoming identified with that content.

- **Mindfulness:** the practice of bringing one's attention to the internal and external experiences occurring in the present moment.

- **Moore's Law**: the observation that the number of transistors in a dense integrated circuit doubles approximately every two years. The observation is named after Gordon E. Moore, the co-founder of Intel and Fairchild Semiconductor, whose 1965 paper described a doubling every year in the number of components per integrated circuit, and projected this rate of growth would continue for at least another decade. In 1975, looking forward to the next decade, he revised the forecast to doubling every two years. This definition has been used to refer to "computing power" or the speed of a computer's CPU (Central Processing Unit) in general.

    As of this writing, Moore's Law has all but been discarded as other factors control the function and usable speed of computers.

- **Nanocomputers**: the logical name for a computer smaller than the microcomputer, which is smaller than the minicomputer.

- **Nondual or Nonduality**: The teaching that suggests that there is only Oneness and that any attempt to fragment or abstract it leads to error. The inquiry of "Neti Neti" – not this and not that – can lead to this realization; sometimes also referred to as the Hindu concept of "Advaita", which refers to the idea that all of the universe is one, essential reality, and that all facets and aspects of the universe are ultimately an expression or appearance of that one reality. Nonduality is the philosophical, spiritual, and scientific understanding of non-separation and fundamental intrinsic Oneness.

    https://www.scienceandnonduality.com/about/nonduality

- **Organic**: matter that has come from a once-living organism, is capable of decay or the product of decay, or is composed of organic compounds or a compound that contains carbon.

- **Panpsychism**: the view that consciousness, mind or soul (psyche) is a universal and primordial feature of all things.

- **Pantheism**: the belief that all of reality is identical with divinity, or that everything composes an all-encompassing, immanent god. Pantheists thus do not believe in a distinct personal or anthropomorphic god.

- **Phi (see Golden Ratio).**

- **Pythagorean Theorem**: also known as Pythagoras' theorem, states that the square of the hypotenuse (the side opposite the right angle) is equal to the sum of the squares of the other two sides. The theorem can be written as an equation relating the lengths of the sides a, b and c, often called the "Pythagorean equation": $a^2 + b^2 = c^2$.

- **Qualia**: individual instances of subjective, conscious experience; what some consider to be individual instances of subjective, conscious experience. Examples of qualia include the pain of a headache, the taste of wine, or the perceived redness of an evening sky. There is no scientific explanation of how such quality of experience can arise within inanimate matter.

- **Software**: that part of a computer system that consists of encoded information or computer instructions.

Bibliography & Additional Resources

Bernal, Martin: *Black Athena*

Black Edwin: *IBM and the Holocaust*

Bhaumik, Mani: *Code Name God*

Brown, Dan: *The Lost Symbol*, (Institute of Noetic Sciences)

Castaneda, Carlos: *The Teachings of Don Juan*

His Holiness the Dalia Lama & Howard C. Cutler, M.D.: *The Art of Happiness*

Damassio, Antonio, *Self Comes to Mind*

Davila, Randy: *The Gnostic Mystery*

de Mello, Anthony SJ & J. Francis Stroud: *Awareness: The Perils and Opportunities of Reality*

Dispenza, Joe: *Evolve Your Brain: The Science of Changing Your Mind*

Dreaver, Jim: *End Your Story, Begin Your Life*

Duhigg, Charles: *The Power of Habit: Why We Do What We Do in Life and Business*

Enriquez, Juan: Video on TED

Gaffney, Rinpoche, Sogyal & Andrew Harvey: *The Tibetan Book of Living and Dying*

Haramein, Nassim: *The Black Whole*

Huxley, Aldous: *The Doors of Perception*

Hofstadter, Douglas: *I Am a Strange Loop*

Lipton, Bruce: *The Biology of Belief*

Malkowski, Edward: *The Spiritual Technology of Ancient Egypt*

Needleman, Jacob: *Why Can't We Be Good?* and *A Sense of the Cosmos*

Pert, Candace: *Molecules of Emotion: The Science Behind Mind-Body Medicine*

Prager, Dennis: *Happiness Is a Serious Problem*

Ruiz, Don Miguel: *The Four Agreements*

Rushkoff, Douglas: *Life Inc.* and *Program or be Programmed*

Schwaller de Lubicz, Rene: *The Temple of Man*

Taleb, Nassim Nicholas: *The Black Swan: Second Edition: The Impact of the Highly Improbable*

Tolle, Eckhart: *A New Earth* and *The Power of Now*

Tompkins, Peter: *Secrets of the Great Pyramid* and *The Secret Life of Plants*

Tompkins, Peter & Harleston Jr., Hugh: *Mysteries of the Mexican Pyramids*

von Daniken, Erik: *Chariots of the Gods*

Zukav, Gary: *The Dancing Wu Li Masters* and *The Seat of the Soul*

(A DVD version of a television special on West's theories was narrated by Charlton Heston)

About the Author

Tom Bunzel is the Technology and Science Columnist for Collective Evolution, a web portal with over 3 million hits per month. He has covered and spoken at the Science and Nonduality Conference and the Superconscious Mind Congress in Puebla, Mexico. As "Professor PowerPoint" he wrote, lectured and taught seminars on business and technology and appeared on Tech TV *Call for Help*.

Bunzel's business-related book for Wiley is *Tools of Engagement: Presenting and Training in a World of Social Media*. *Presence of Mind: Journey to a New Operating System* combines his fascination with technology with spirituality. Other books include *Solving the PowerPoint Predicament: Using Digital Media for Effective Communication*, a detailed, project-oriented approach to creating effective presenting. A full bio and listing of his books is available on Amazon.

Tom currently lives in Las Vegas, Nevada where he's also Director of Corporate Communications for Community Vision Inc.

Facebook: Tom Bunzel Author

LinkedIn: Tom Bunzel

Email: tom.bunzel@communityvision.com

This book was published by:

Azure Reading Books

848 North Rainbow Bl.

Suite A111

Las Vegas, Nevada 89107

USA, Earth

admin@azurereadingbooks.com

www.azurereadingbooks.com

Contact Azure Reading Books for information regarding speaking engagements or teaching seminars.

ATTENTION CORPORATIONS, SCHOOL DISTRICTS, UNIVERSITIES, and PROFESSIONAL ORGANIZATIONS:

Quantity discounts are available on bulk purchases of this book for instructional purposes. Please contact us for more information.

Index

A

AATCAGGGACCC, 32-33, 42
abstraction, 81, 183, 194
acai, 84
Acapulco, 139
activate, 40, 82, 84, 87, 154
actualize, 71, 188
addiction, 143, 165
addictive, 149, 166, 177
Adenine, 38
Adonai, 65
Advaita, 181, 186, 221
affair, 102, 139
afterlife, 70
agreements, 117-118, 131, 184, 224
aha, 51, 213
algorithm, 94, 211, 219
alienation, 179, 214
Aliens, 104
Alzheimer, 109-110
Amsterdam, 138
analysis, 25, 30
animacy, 102
animals, 5, 168
anthropomorphic, 90, 106, 120, 222
anxiety, 86, 134, 164, 169, 172, 184, 187, 189
anxious, 136, 176, 189, 192
Arab, 172
Arabian, 48, 66
archeology, 104, 119, 184
arithmetical, 24
aroused, 140, 150
asceticism, 121
astronomer, 23, 104, 115, 199, 212
atheists, 90-91, 105
Athena, 223
Atlantis, 75
Auschwitz, 131
Autobiographical, 202
automate, 15, 137
awaken, 17, 70, 122, 137, 165, 172, 201, 213
awe, 2, 67, 105, 152
Aztecs, 119

INDEX

B

Babbage, 24-25, 27, 57
Bach, 94
bachelor, 82
bacteria, 36
baggage, 146
Bain, 1
balls, 138
Barnet, 1
BDSM, 139, 141, 144, 148-149, 151, 155, 219
Benavides, 119
Berman, 108
Bernal, 223
Bernoulli, 25
Betsy, 24-25
Beverly, 129
Bhaumik, 223
bi, 172
Bible, 86, 219
billiard, 157
Biocentrism, 66, 108, 121, 203, 219
biochemical, 33, 38, 54, 83-84, 200, 217
Biomimetics, 219
Biomimicry, 101, 219
biophysics, 109
bioplasmic, 210
Bleep, 192
bondage, 139, 143-144, 219

Bruce, 55, 109, 223
Buckminster, 54
Buddhism, 120, 189
bunk, 131
Byron, 63-64

C

cacao, 84
Cancun, 119
Candace, 223
Caribbean, 141
Carleton, 9
Carlo, 158
Carlos, 223
Carolina, 161
Cartesian, 19, 24
Cas, 35-36
casino, 158, 165-167
Castaneda, 223
causal, 60, 96, 159
chaos, 36, 58, 103, 122, 130, 158
Chariots, 224
Charles, 24-25, 57, 223
Charlotte, 161
Charlton, 224
chastity, 144
Cheops, 104
Chicago, 176, 207
Chichen, 119
Chopra, 55, 109-110, 113, 211-212, 216

INDEX

Christianity, 70, 120
Christians, 91
Christopher, 36
Chrome, 51, 54
chromosomes, 30
Circe, 166
cognition, 1, 145, 201, 203, 217
comet, 75
computerhistory, 24
contraception, 138
Coon, 169
Copernican, 201, 204
cosmic, 106, 201
cosmology, 88, 120, 203
Cosmos, 18, 70, 91, 103, 199-201, 214-215, 217, 223
Costanza, 193
CPU, 221
Craig, 30
Creationism, 91, 219
creator, 30, 122
CRISPR, 35-36
crystallize, 19, 89, 139, 178, 184
curvy, 143
Cutler, 223
Cytosine, 38

D

Dalia, 223
Dallery, 9
Damasio, 201-203
Damassio, 223
Dan, 223
Daniken, 104, 224
Darko, 9
Dass, 175
David, 61, 76, 110, 190, 198
Davila, 223
Davis, 35
Dawkins, 91
Debra, 9
debug, 15, 195, 212
Deepak, 55, 109-110, 113, 211-212, 216
Deism, 91, 106, 219
Deity, 92
demons, 132, 147
DeNicola, 1
Dennis, 224
Deoxyribonucleic, 219
depression, 82, 164
Descartes, 19, 53, 214
deviated, 135
devotees, 151
disease, 35, 109-110, 138, 216
Dispenza, 110, 192-193, 205, 223

divine, 1, 71, 219
divinity, 222
dogma, 212, 220
dominance, 75, 138-139, 143-144, 148, 219
dominatrix, 141
Donald, 177
dope, 162
Douglas, 15, 61, 80, 94, 194, 223-224
Dreaver, 9, 174, 223
Dresser, 48-49
dualistic, 107
Duality, 121
Duhigg, 223

E

Eagelman, 199
Ebola, 6, 33
Eckhart, 12, 17, 22, 49, 63, 77, 82, 87-88, 103, 121, 125, 129, 139, 145, 155, 172-173, 177, 181, 184, 186-187, 198, 200-201, 206-209, 213-216, 224
Edward, 223
Edwin, 223
Ego, 81-82, 86-88, 94, 103, 150, 159, 165-166, 177-178, 182, 189, 201, 213, 216
egocentric, 203

egoic, 86, 206
egoism, 214
Egypt, 120, 223
Egyptian, 70, 91-93, 104, 184, 211
Einstein, 106, 181-183
Eliot, 118
embryo, 49
Emerson, 91, 106
emptiness, 141
Enriquez, 18, 32-34, 40, 42, 47, 61, 66, 211, 223
Entscheidungsproblem, 28
Epigenetics, 17, 46, 51, 55, 61, 66, 76, 84, 109, 121-122, 210, 216, 220
equanimity, 172, 220
erection, 152
Erik, 104, 224
Escher, 94
Euclid, 97
evolution, 1, 17, 87, 103, 112, 122, 202, 210, 225
evolutionary, 103, 201, 203, 215-216
EXE, 32, 42, 50
executable, 32, 50, 147
execute, 32, 42, 46, 196, 217
extraterrestrials, 70

INDEX

F

Fairchild, 221
Feminism, 139, 143
fetal, 12
fetish, 143, 151
Fibonacci, 91, 93, 96, 98, 101, 103-104, 194, 196, 211, 220
Floyd, 198
fluorescing, 48
Fundamentalism, 91, 111, 220

G

Gaffney, 223
galactic, 17, 55, 203, 217
Galileo, 16, 92, 94
gambler, 162
Gargiulo, 2, 9
gays, 141
Genome, 30, 35, 85, 216
genotype, 220
geology, 122
geometric, 29, 158, 194
Geometry, 6, 91-94, 98-100, 211
Ghezzi, 9
Gibson, 199
Giza, 23, 104
Gleick, 103
Gnostic, 70, 223
Gnostics, 120-121
Gödel, 94, 97, 102
Gordon, 221
Graham, 1, 75, 104
gratification, 154
Greeks, 92, 98, 104, 181, 211
Guanine, 38
Gurdjieff, 70, 81-82, 88, 100, 120-122, 130, 188-189, 201, 213

H

Hameroff, 74
Hancock, 1, 75, 104
Haramein, 223
Harleston, 224
Harvey, 223
Hebrew, 65, 220
Heston, 224
heterosexual, 143
Hexadecimal, 46
hieroglyphs, 23, 91
Hindu, 221
Hinduism, 120
Hofstadter, 61, 80, 84, 87, 94-99, 102-103, 194-196, 223
Holiness, 223
Hollerith, 27
Holocaust, 128, 178-179, 223
homeopathic, 127

INDEX

homeostasis, 201
Hood, 6, 39
hooker, 138, 141
housecat, 48
Howard, 223
Hoyle, 115, 197
HTML, 6, 33, 37, 43, 46, 51, 54, 220
Huxley, 77, 223

I
IBM, 15, 27, 210, 223
Incognito, 76, 198-199
interbreeding, 202
Israel, 172
Italian, 93, 104
Itza, 119

J
Jeffreys, 9, 62, 88, 172, 180, 190, 205
Jews, 27, 68
Judaism, 6, 68, 220
Jung, 144
Juric, 9

K
Kabbalah, 68, 70, 220
Kabbalist, 220
Kafatos, 75
Kernan, 9
Kiloby, 165

Kippur, 68
Knoepfler, 35
Krishnamurti, 195
Kumar, 1
Kurt, 97
Kurzweil, 99

L
Lama, 223
Lane, 208
Lanza, 66, 80, 108, 113, 203, 219
Lascaux, 23
Lennox, 1, 9
Leonardo, 93, 95
Li, 224
Lipton, 55, 109, 223
Liquorman, 61, 206
Lovelace, 24-25, 27-29, 57
Lubicz, 224

M
Maat, 184
Maher, 91
Maine, 169
Malkowski, 223
Manhattan, 137
Marie, 9
marijuana, 140
Martin, 223
Masochism, 139, 219
Mayan, 119, 162

INDEX

Mekubbal, 220
Mello, 223
Menas, 75
Mexican, 119, 224
Mexico, 119, 225
Michaels, 9
microbiome, 216
Miehls, 2
Miguel, 117, 224
Miles, 87
Miller, 9
Milton, 1
mimicry, 31
Mindfulness, 221
MIT, 35-36
monotheism, 17
Monte, 158
Moore, 99, 101, 221
Morgan, 2
MSCONFIG, 78
mutation, 215
myopia, 212
myopic, 74
mysticism, 69, 86, 121
mythology, 166

N

Nanocomputers, 30, 221
nanotechnology, 210
NASA, 111-112, 114
Nassim, 223-224
Nazi, 27, 131, 133, 145

Needleman, 9, 103, 120, 214-215, 217, 223
Nefesh, 70
Neshamah, 70
Neter, 184
Neters, 91, 184
Neti, 221
Newtonian, 84, 89
Nicolai, 120
Nile, 91, 184
Noetic, 223
Nondual, 61, 181, 186, 195, 206, 221
Nonduality, 6, 74-75, 106-107, 110, 221, 225

O

Oneness, 221
ontogeny, 1
ontologically, 74
ontology, 108
Oprah, 17
Ouspensky, 81-82, 88, 120-121

P

Palindromic, 36
Panpsychism, 57, 222
Pantheism, 91, 106, 222
Pavlov, 15
PBS, 77, 201
Pert, 223

INDEX

phenotype, 30, 220
phylogeny, 1
Plato, 73-75, 86, 91
Platonic, 74, 105
Platonism, 75
Prager, 224
Puebla, 225
Pulitzer, 94
Pyramid, 26, 57, 91, 93, 104, 119-120, 224
Pythagoras, 91, 95, 222
Pythagorean, 104, 222

Q

Qualia, 110, 113, 171, 197, 203, 216-217, 222
Quantum, 18, 30, 84, 94, 106, 110, 121-122, 181, 201, 210-212

R

Ratio, 95-96, 104, 220, 222
Ravi, 54
Renaissance, 93
RGB, 37, 42, 45, 216
Rinpoche, 223
Riviera, 138
Robbins, 193
Ruach, 70
Rudolfo, 119
Rudolph, 109
Rudy, 55, 109, 216
Ruiz, 117, 224
Rupert, 100, 107, 110, 195, 200
Rushkoff, 15, 224

S

Salzmann, 188
sandcat, 48-49, 66
Sanskrit, 119
Schwaller, 224
Scientism, 103, 121, 212
Scott, 165
scripture, 91, 220
Seinfeld, 193
Semiconductor, 221
Semite, 199
Shankar, 54
Shapero, 9
Sharkskin, 101
Smith, 2
Sogyal, 223
Spira, 100, 107, 110, 195, 200
Stahl, 48
Stecchini, 104
Stevens, 87
Stroud, 223
Stuart, 74
suicide, 63
Superconscious, 225
Swan, 224

INDEX

Swihart, 9
Switzerland, 179
synagogue, 68
synapses, 200

T
Tagore, 181, 183
Taleb, 224
Tanzi, 55, 109-110, 216
TED, 32, 223
Tesla, 120
theology, 1
theopedia, 219
Thoreau, 91, 106
Thymine, 38
Tibetan, 223
Tolle, 12, 17, 22, 49, 63, 77, 82, 87-88, 103, 121, 125, 139, 145, 155, 172-173, 177, 181, 184, 186-187, 198, 200-201, 206-208, 214-215, 224
Toltec, 118
Tompkins, 104, 119, 224
transsexual, 152
Turing, 28, 99
Twitter, 148

U
unscientific, 103

V
Venus, 140
Vienna, 157
Vinci, 93, 95
Voigt, 36

W
Watson, 27, 210
Watts, 195
Wayne, 61, 206
Webopedia, 196
Whitman, 91, 106
Wiley, 225
Winfrey, 17
Wu, 224
WWII, 141

Y
Yom, 68
York, 161, 179
Yorker, 24-25
YouTube, 182
Yucatan, 119
Yup, 157

Z
Zukav, 224

Notes

Notes

Notes

CPSIA information can be obtained
at www.ICGtesting.com
Printed in the USA
LVOW13s1505120117
520742LV00028B/827/P